Molyneaux:
The Long View

This book is due for return on or before the last date shown below.

Molyneaux:
The Long View

by

ANN PURDY

Greystone Books
1989

To Willie and Jim – many thanks

Published in 1989
by Greystone Books Ltd
Antrim, Northern Ireland

© Ann Purdy, 1989

ISBN 1 870157 06 0

Cover design and illustrations by Rodney Miller Associates

Printed by W. & G. Baird Ltd
at the Greystone Press, Antrim, Northern Ireland

Contents

The authors and publisher are indebted to the following sources of reference:

Time and Chance, James Callaghan – Collins/Fontana.
British Government and Politics, R. M. Punnett – Gower.
Northern Ireland: A Political Directory 1968–88, W. D. Flackes, Sydney Elliott – The Blackstaff Press.
John Hume – Statesman of the Troubles, Barry White – The Blackstaff Press.
The Fall of the Northern Ireland Executive, Paddy Devlin – Gill and Macmillan.
Northern Ireland: A Personal Perspective, Merlyn Rees.
Northern Ireland: Who is to Blame? Andrew Boyd, Mercier Press.
The Irish Triangle/Conflict in Northern Ireland, Roger H. Hull.
Faulkner: Memoirs of a Statesman.
The Ulster Unionist Party 1882/73, John Harbinson – The Blackstaff Press.
The Factory of Grievances, Devolved Government in Northern Ireland, 1921/39.
Ian Paisley: Voice of Protestant Ulster, Clifford Smyth.
The Lives of Enoch Powell, Patrick Cosgrave.
Hansard, the official records of the House of Commons 1970/88 and Hansard, the official records of the Northern Ireland Assembly 1982/86.

Foreword

Shortly after the Prior Assembly got off the ground in November 1982, Fortnight magazine ran a poll. It was not the usual gleaning of views from the public on a certain issue but amongst the Press corps ensconced at Stormont. Everyone, including myself, was asked for their views on the politicians who were being displayed in front of us in the chamber.

Needless to say there were a few very scathing and cynical remarks made. But there was one which ran through the Jim Molyneaux "form" sheet. He was a gentleman. It is still the same today.

I had met him for the first time as would-be Ulster Unionist Assemblymen handed in their nominations for the South Antrim seats. He was obviously there as party leader and the sitting member for the constituency. I asked the usual pre-election questions and then we had a few minutes of small talk.

For some reason we began to discuss the duties of an MP and he regaled to me the story of a woman constituent who telephoned him just as he sat down to his Christmas dinner. She had telephoned "Mr Molyneaux" to complain about the telegraph pole which was obstructing the clear view out of her front room window and was demanding to know as to what he was going to do about it. He politely asked her had it gone up that morning to which he received "No, of course not, six months ago". The MP, in turn, then asked would she mind if he took his Christmas dinner first before pursuing the matter.

It was the way he told this story which struck me. He did not retell it in a sneering manner and while he obviously saw the funny side of it, he understood, without saying anything to me, that maybe the woman was lonely and had no one else to talk to that Christmas Day.

This is a side of Jim Molyneaux no one generally sees. He has never fitted the mould of Northern Ireland politicians. He is a quiet, shy man which has made him easy prey for the "Paisley puppet" and "Powell poodle" slogans. Nothing could be further from the truth. He has a shrewdness and cunning few take the time to see. As a former Secretary of State Merlyn Rees noted: "A much underrated politician".

vii

He has a silent fortitude which stems from war experience and which has helped cast this "cold fish" appearance which spurred one party colleague on to note: "The trouble about you leader is that we never know what you are thinking".

I hope this conglomeration of conversations will give some insight into the man and what he does think. This is primarily him speaking and why it has been carried through in this manner is simply to show that there is a face and personality behind the cold slab image which I have no need to embellish with "well-informed" criticism or an in depth analysis of certain political situations. It is simply to set out aspects of Jim Molyneaux's character and his views on a variety of scenes which have not been known before. It is entirely up to the individual whether or not they accept them.

He has been described as inept, a weakling, too conservative and someone who has no vision of the future in Northern Ireland. In contrast, he has held together a party which was practically dead in the mid-1970s and which still tends to enjoy its internal wranglings being washed in public. In spite of the easy analysis that he is overshadowed by Paisley, he saw his party gain seats to the detriment of the DUP in the 1989 local government elections. In typical fashion afterwards he did not laud it over the other political leader.

It was for the reason that few take the time to find out more about the man behind the "faceless" Molyneaux image that this project began. The portrayal is always of someone who speaks in gobbledegook and yet he likes nothing better than chatting with party workers or any other group of people in some wee hall "up country".

This is where his strength lies. As the first leader of the Ulster Unionist Party who does not come from the "big house" Jim Molyneaux has always relied on the views and opinions of those who, as far as he is concerned, matter the most. When criticism of his leadership has been thick and heavy he always enjoys gauging what "ordinary" people think and usually comes away with a spring in his step.

In contrast to the popular image of this nondescript wee man, he has a wicked sense of humour, is a great mimic, is generous to a fault and still takes time to sing in the church choir.

When I went to London to interview several people about Molyneaux, I could not believe the warmth and high regard he was held in by English politicians. No one raised a word of criticism about his character, even if they felt he had been wrong in his political judgement and while former Secretary of State Jim Prior wondered how I was going to get a book out of such a subject, he emphasised that he had only given me of his time because he regarded Molyneaux so highly.

But the comment which, for me, sums up Jim Molyneaux best comes from the former Prime Minister Lord Callaghan. When I wrote to him asking for his views he recommended that I read his memoirs but he added "you could not write about a nicer man".

May I take this opportunity to thank Mr John Kennedy and his staff Helen and George at the Assembly Library, Parliament Buildings, Stormont, and Norah, Helen and Roy at Ulster Unionist Headquarters who all never complained when I asked for yet another factual verification.

Ann Purdy,
Belfast, October 1989.

1. Rally

On a sharp, bright November afternoon in 1985, his black rimmed glasses perched on the end of his nose and battling against a faulty loudspeaker system, the leader of the Ulster Unionist Party told an audience of more than 200,000 in Belfast city centre that it was expected of rally speakers to conclude by raising their audience to fever pitch.

Instead, with the City Hall as a back drop and surrounded by Unionist MPs, Jim Molyneaux informed the gathering that he would do the opposite.

"The situation is too serious. The occasion is too solemn to do other than invite you to prepare yourselves for the long hard road to success. It will require staying power such as we have never known.

So take home with you and remember these words: 'Grant us to know that it is not the beginning but the continuing of the same, until it be thoroughly finished which yieldeth the True Glory'."

It was a deliberate downbeat ending to a speech to the largest crowd he had ever addressed in his political life. He received a polite response before a massive roar went running through the audience for the next speaker – Ian Paisley. But Molyneaux, in a very calculated, understated fashion, had told the crowd what they had to hear – not what they wanted to hear. A fight was on their hands and it would not be won after one round.

It was November 23 – eight days after the signing of the Anglo-Irish Agreement in Hillsborough Castle between the British Prime Minister Margaret Thatcher and the Irish Taoiseach Dr Garret FitzGerald. It heralded a new relationship between the two sovereign governments and brought the largest Unionist storm of protest on to the streets of Northern Ireland since the 1912 Home Rule crisis.

The Belfast city centre "Dump the Deal" rally as labelled by one newspaper, was an even larger gathering than witnessed for the signing of the Ulster Covenant. It had been organised in haste with advertisements only appearing for it a few days earlier. Even the organisers could not hide their delight at the size of the crowd – in spite of one Dublin newspaper later estimating it at 35,000.

1

The wave of opposition in the Unionist community to the Agreement had rolled right across the country. They believed, rightly or wrongly, that the accord struck by London and Dublin, undermined their position within the UK and for the first time ever Dublin had a direct input into the internal affairs of Northern Ireland.

It meant that many "average" Unionists who had not been involved in any protests before were outraged and joined in the march to Belfast city centre. The Orange Order, always a cornerstone in a loyalist numbers' game, called on all members to attend and the vast majority did. A line of buses along the nearby M1 motorway stretched for almost six miles.

But this immediate reaction of opposition amongst Unionists masked a confusion within their political parties as to how they could make the Agreement impotent. Their senior members, in spite of continually reiterating grave worries and concerns about the Anglo-Irish process had been left out in the cold by the two governments. They had been shunted on to the sidings and now they wanted to get an opposition campaign on to the main track.

Just three days before the historic signing at the former Governor of Northern Ireland's official residence, Molyneaux had been told by a senior Cabinet figure that such an agreement was unthinkable. He flatly refused to accept Molyneaux's warnings of what was to come and told the Unionist leader curtly: "We cannot make an agreement with a nation which obviously claims part of the territory of the United Kingdom".

However the marginalising of the Unionist leaders had made their protests of pending gloom and doom ineffectual. They could only stand on the sidelines and watch the two governments build up a controlled game of politics and diplomacy.

Molyneaux could only describe Paisley and his views' as "advice to the Government" in a statement made at a press conference in Enniskillen on November 4. He said the two men had a duty to advise the British Government and the people of the Irish Republic that the previous ten months of secret dealings had increased tensions between the Unionist and Nationalist people in Northern Ireland.

He told the seven reporters who had turned up at the venue that any outcome of the Anglo-Irish talks which went beyond normal arrangements between sovereign states would "obliterate for decades the patient endeavours which had been giving hope for a stable Northern Ireland up to a year ago". The press conference had been designed for the Dublin audience although no reporter from the Irish capital was present.

Molyneaux placed great store by the Irish Government's emphasis on the "unique" relationship between Dublin and London and maintained that Unionists too wanted to see it made real. But, he told the small band, before such a relationship was achieved there had to be the building of a normal one. However he recognised that he was in a shadow boxing predicament. He and Paisley, while having had two meetings with the Prime Minister and reading the rising swell of press speculation, still did not know the framework on which the Agreement was to be hung and the Government's vagueness neutered the Unionist leaders. They could shout all they wanted to, no one was listening and there was a prevalent attitude in both London and Dublin that at least without the Unionists talks could progress.

On November 13 Upper Bann MP Harold McCusker asked the House of Commons Speaker Bernard Weatherill if the Prime Minister was going to make a statement on the continuing Anglo-Irish talks as the Dublin newspapers that morning had given the precise details of the looming agreement.

"Is it not despicable that honourable members from Northern Ireland learn of their betrayal and the diminishing of their citizenship from a newspaper published in Dublin?" he asked. This was followed by a supplementary from Molyneaux: "Are you aware that the Irish Government intends to circulate the full text of the agreement tomorrow? Is it not intolerable that this House will be kept in the dark until at least next week? Is it not possible for the Leader of the House to ensure that the Secretary of State for Northern Ireland makes a full and comprehensive statement tomorrow when he answers Northern Ireland questions?"

Such questions may have proved that the Unionists were at least aware of the situation but answers in the House the following day showed just how isolated they were. Less than 24 hours before the helicopters bringing the two Prime Ministers' landed on the lawn at Hillsborough, in oral answers to questions the Law and Order Minister Nicholas Scott told Molyneaux that he may have heard things on radio or television or have read about them in newspapers. If, he said, there was to be any such agreement as was rumoured, then he recommended to the House to read its terms carefully and to listen to any statement that was to be made to the House of Commons.

The Secretary of State Tom King suggested to members that any negotiations between sovereign states inevitably had to be conditioned with some degree of confidentiality Tory back bencher Viscount Cranbourne then asked the Prime Minister, in spite of her busy day, if she knew if any member of the American administration or an official of it was already aware of the terms of the Anglo-Irish Agreement. Margaret Thatcher said the member would understand that she could not comment further on whether or not any agreement would or would not be signed.

Molyneaux tried. On a point of order he asked: "In practically every answer about the Anglo-Irish Agreement the Secretary of State for Northern Ireland and the Prime Minister advised us to wait to see the contents of that agreement and to study the statement. Is it not intolerable that the House of Commons should be the last to hear the contents of that agreement which was widely published 48 hours ago"?

But the Agreement was ready to be signed and the Unionists remained in splendid isolation. Molyneaux is an uncharacteristic Unionist leader. He is quiet and shy. Self-effacing, he has never been known to create a scene. He enjoys meeting and chatting to people on an informal basis but has never been distinguished in his public speaking. He has an incredible well of self-reliance and rarely shows anger. Unlike other Northern Ireland politicians he does not make an instant pronouncement on a particular situation. This leaves him open to the criticism that he avoids confronting the obvious. He would argue that it is better to continue behind the scenes diplomacy than creating or adding to circumstances which will be forgotten about in 24 hours.

Because of this deliberate decision Molyneaux tends to stand back and is enabled to see around the corner. It is why he warned the wider Unionist community that they had a long struggle on their hands and that the Agreement would not disappear overnight. However it does not explain why, because of this knowing, that he and Paisley only began their rearguard action against the London/Dublin pact four months before its signing. By then most of the groundwork on the accord had been done and the Prime Minister was confident enough in the process to change her top man at Stormont Castle from Douglas Hurd who was promoted to the Home Office, to Employment Secretary Tom King. Only days after his arrival in early September he was able to point out that already that year ministers from the two governments had met at least 20 times.

The Unionist response to the widespread rumblings with no confirmation was to set up a joint working party. It was to co-ordinate Unionist policy and set out its case. There were six members on it – from the Ulster Unionists there were Upper Bann MP Harold McCusker, party secretary Frank Millar and barrister Peter Smith. Their contemporaries from the DUP were deputy leader Peter Robinson, press officer Sammy Wilson and Fermanagh Assemblyman Ivan Foster.

The move prompted the Unionist inclined morning newspaper the *News Letter* to move its leader column to the front page on August 3. It noted: "We support unreservedly the decision by the leaders of Ulster Unionism to appoint a joint working party whose responsibility it will be to suggest strategies by which Ulster's interests within the UK can best be protected. Their joint statement makes it plain that even a consultative role for the Republic in Northern Ireland affairs would be a violation of the Government's assurance of Ulster's right to self determination and would strike at Ulster's integrity".

The two leaders, the previous day, had expressed their deep disquiet about the "nature and purpose" of secret negotiations between the Government and that of the Irish Republic. They also warned that if the secrecy went on unchecked then "constitutional Unionism" could be rendered impotent. The two men admitted that their calls for candour had received no response and so as a counter move a working party would be created. It would, they said, analyse the current situation to anticipate the shape of events in the coming months and to suggest the strategy or strategies by which Ulster's interests within the UK could be protected.

They coldly warned that because they had been kept in the dark they had no option but to prepare for the worst. It was rather like shutting the door after the horse had bolted. The roots of the Anglo-Irish Agreement had already taken in the soil of the New Ireland Forum more than 20 months previously thanks to the untiring work of SDLP leader John Hume.

The Forum began its proceedings in Dublin in May 1983 as a conference of the four main nationalist parties – Fianna Fail, Fine Gael, the Irish Labour Party and the SDLP. Its aim was to work out an agreed nationalist approach to a Northern Ireland settlement. It was Hume's sheer determination which saw the conference hold its first public question and answer session in September of that year, although he had been working towards an Anglo-Irish approach to Northern Ireland since the doomed Humphrey Atkins round table conference. Even then he demanded that there be an Irish dimension to the talks and held separate party meetings with the Secretary of State on the matter.

The Forum held plenary sessions for the rest of 1983 and early 1984. Unionist policy was simple – there was no acceptance of invitations to address the gathering and no written submissions even of explanation as to why they would not attend. The two parties maintained their well-worn cry of no structured Dublin involvement in the internal affairs of Northern Ireland. Only the Church of Ireland made a formal submission and the two McGimpsey brothers, Christopher and Michael, broke Ulster Unionist policy to give oral evidence. However, their party, just one month before the Forum Report was published in May, unveiled its own paper which was eventually endorsed as party policy.

The main thrust of "The Way Forward" was equal rights for all British citizens; however it emphasised that for both communities in Ulster to work together they had to realise that the best solution was to live within a Northern Ireland context. It stressed that it was the responsibility of the majority to persuade the minority that Northern Ireland was also theirs. It proposed administrative devolution inside the Province with limited powers over local government but without an executive. It guaranteed the minority an influential role in committees, a Bill of Rights and an "Irish dimension". It promoted widespread interest but little response from the SDLP. Its eyes were still firmly fixed on the Dublin gathering whose work appeared in print soon afterwards.

All of the participating parties made it clear that their first preference was for a unitary 32 county state. They also, however, put forward the options of a federal arrangement and joint authority exercised by both London and Dublin. Ulster Secretary Jim Prior said he found the report's account of the British position as "one sided and unacceptable" and he reiterated that the Thatcher administration would continue to support Northern Ireland as part of the UK as long as the majority so wished. The Unionist response was predictable – they regarded it as an interference and Paisley made a midnight foray into Dublin to stick a poster noting that "Ulster is British" on the General Post Office building.

The Prime Minister gave her views on the report in the famous Chequers outburst of mid-November. The two heads of government met in the British politician's country residence for the second meeting within the framework of the British Irish Intergovernmental Council. The Irish Taoiseach Garret FitzGerald put forward the three options culled from the Dublin deliberations and received the succinct reply of "out, out, out". It has been suggested that this had been fuelled by the previous month's IRA bombing of the Brighton hotel in which she had been staying for the Conservative Party Conference and which killed three people including an MP. FitzGerald was deeply hurt and told party colleagues that her remarks had been "gratuitously offensive" but she was unremorseful to the delight of Unionists.

However the agreed communique issued afterwards committed London and Dublin to reflecting the identities of both communities "in the structures and process of Northern Ireland". The Prime Minister told the House of Commons on November 20 that the two politicians had had a "thorough and realistic exchange of views" on developments in relation to Northern Ireland and between the two governments. She continued: "We agreed that it was a major interest of both our countries as well as both the majority and minority communities in Northern Ireland that there should be lasting peace and stability there".

The leader of the Ulster Unionist Party rose from his seat on the Opposition benches and told her: "May I congratulate the Prime Minister on the courage and clear sightedness that she showed in taking the Government off the treadmill of initiatives which, in the past, have been the cause of so much turmoil? Will she consider phasing out summits of this type which also add to instability?"

Mrs Thatcher replied that everyone wanted to find a political framework which was acceptable to both communities in Northern Ireland. She admitted that this had yet to be achieved and hoped the political parties in the Province would play a constructive part in trying to seek it. But the damage had been done by her blustery "out, out, out" comments and Dublin was deeply offended. Worse still, the mandarins of the Foreign and Northern Ireland Offices could not believe their ears, Molyneaux had a particular insight into how angry they were. A friend, with no connections with politics in London, spoke to a Foreign Office official soon after Christmas and asked what sort of a holiday he had had.

The reply came back that it had been miserable. He had worked overtime through the festive season trying to "undo the damage that bloody woman has done". The Unionist leader relayed this to his close friend and adviser the South Down MP Enoch Powell who recognised the significance of the diligent Yuletide work.

"The Foreign Office, not the Northern Ireland Office, was aghast at what the Prime Minister had said and the reaction there had been to it in the Irish Republic and America. Therefore the Foreign Office had to ensure, with the support of the Northern Ireland Office, of trying to heal the wounds and of applying the maximum pressure to reverse the situation". Molyneaux realised the officials would not go to the Prime Minister to inform her of the damage but instead set about working on the joint communique and the commitment the two governments had made. A working party was formed and began the process which eventually produced the framework for the Agreement, spurred on by

the Foreign and Cabinet Offices. By February 1985, the Prime Minister
was already referring to the excellent relations she had with the Irish
Premier.

Molyneaux had enjoyed what he saw as reassurances in the "out, out,
out" declaration. But by the Easter adjournment debate of March 26 he
had begun to wake up to the reality that Unionist politicians were being
excluded from some grand scheme. He told the House that the Prime
Minister, in her November statement, had made it crystal clear that the
principle of self-determination made it necessary to reject the three
options of the Forum Report. He claimed that because of this there was
evidence across Northern Ireland of a dramatic change in attitudes.
Unionists and Nationalists had recognised the futility of squabbling
about what was going to happen and began to wonder how they could
co-operate in making Ulster a better place for everyone.

But he noted that such stability was being put at risk and he cited a
speech made by Dr FitzGerald the previous week. The Taoiseach had
played host to a lunch which was attended by the Northern Ireland
Secretary Douglas Hurd and Foreign Secretary Sir Geoffrey Howe.
Afterwards Dr FitzGerald had said that they were all working on novel
and far reaching proposals for joint authority over Northern Ireland.
Molyneaux continued: "I recognise that the House is not responsible
for any of these activities but the House is entitled to know the views of
those who are accountable to it – in this case, the Northern Ireland
Ministers. Everything that they have said over the past week has been
so ambiguous that it may have been better left unsaid".

"The instability thus created may not strike some right hon. and hon.
Members as being very important, but the crying shame is that all that
has been achieved in the past five months will be set at naught. The
modest success in persuading citizens of Northern Ireland of all
aspirations that their future is secure and their path known will be
extinguished". He warned that disaster would only be avoided if there
was a clear reiteration of her statement and that diplomatic double talk
was ignored.

But it was Molyneaux and Paisley who were being ignored by the
Anglo-Irish draftsmen. It was they who were being left out in the cold
and were absolutely powerless to act. They could only lobby and air
their disquiet in speeches. It does not, however, clarify why they only
began their campaign that August. Surely, if Molyneaux realised as
early as the February of 1985 that the diplomats on both sides of the
Irish Sea were drafting the Agreement he should have acted sooner. His
peculiar characteristic of being able to have a "long view" and of

recognising the eventual outcome of a policy even before it has left the drawing board failed on this occasion. Maybe he placed too much store by the Prime Minister's "crystal clear" declaration.

He returned to issuing a warning signal in the summer adjournment debate on July 24. Again he condemned the continuing leaks from the Anglo-Irish talks. But this time he was able to list three muted proposals put forward by the Dublin negotiating team. They were the suggestion that Dublin judges share benches in Belfast; the UDR's part-time members would be phased out and the third was the re-routing of loyalist parades. The examples, he said, were wholly at variance with the Government's earlier rejection of joint control or shared sovereignty.

"Ulster people see all of those as the first fruits of the Anglo-Irish secret talks, costly fruits they are and costly they will prove to be. The cost has been the greatest loss of confidence in Northern Ireland Ministers since the ill-fated Sunningdale agreement." He appealed to the Northern Ireland Office Ministers to desist from encouraging a monsoon of leaks, rumours, proposals, studies, deals and initiatives. "To those Ministers who have plunged the Province into a state of unbelievable political confusion, we on this bench say for God's sake, face up to the consequences of your indiscretions. On behalf of all who wish to preserve the democratic process, I suggest, as did Clem Attlee before me, that a period of silence from them would be welcome."

Nine days later the two leaders announced the creation of their joint working party. Within weeks it had drawn up a document "Unionism, a Policy for All the People" and recommended to the two chiefs who did not sit in on its meetings, that they should seek an early audience with the Prime Minister. There were hurdles to jump over diary dates but Friday August 30 at 8.00 pm was agreed. They had already warned Mrs Thatcher, in a letter two days earlier, that the people of Northern Ireland were profoundly anxious about the secrecy surrounding the Anglo-Irish talks. They highlighted that any proposal for increased Anglo-Irish co-operation had to be suspect given the Republic's claim to the territory of Northern Ireland which was, they asserted, a repudiation of its right to self-determination and called on the Government to challenge the Dublin administration to withdraw this claim. The two men said this was an essential prerequisite to greater friendship, co-operation and understanding. Thanks to the working party document they also were able to present the Prime Minister with their alternative to the talks. This said that if UK sovereignty remained undiminished and provided the Republic's territorial claim was withdrawn, they would be willing to contribute to a process of British/Irish discussions and co-operation on two fronts. The first would be as members of a newly formed Government of Northern Ireland, meeting with opposite numbers in the Republic's Government to consider matters of mutual interest and concern within a range of respective departmental responsibilities. The second was as members of a devolved government comprising part of a UK delegation to talk to the Irish Government about matters of "mutual interest". Their sting in the tail was to criticise the SDLP for its continual veto over internal political development and a denial of local democracy.

Within 48 hours they faced the Prime Minister and Douglas Hurd over a coffee table in 10 Downing Street. The meeting lasted 30 minutes and went unnoticed by the press until it was taken up the following Monday. There was a vagueness about it which Molyneaux believes was not deliberate on Thatcher's part.

"We supplemented the document we put forward by suggesting to the Prime Minister the unworkability of that which we had been reading about. She did not tell us anything. Both she and Hurd listened diligently, nodded now and then and took notes." During the discussion Molyneaux raised the Dublin based report about an Irish judge sitting in Belfast. He remembers the Prime Minister's reaction: "It was the one section of the meeting where she did seem to respond with a flash of her eyes. She did not react but I felt, sitting opposite her, that we had touched on a raw nerve. I got the impression that my suggestion was the first time someone had put the proposal to her. Other than that we did not get very far, we simply said we hoped she would listen to our views and that we would meet again".

The two Unionist leaders next inkling of what was to come came from the Conservative Party chairman Norman Tebbit. They had asked for a meeting after Tebbit's deputy, millionaire writer Jeffrey Archer, had said he hoped that some day Ireland would be united. The immediate reason for the appointment was quickly resolved but Tebbit, a member of an ad hoc Cabinet committee, went on to suggest that the two men were not going to like all that was soon going to appear as Government policy.

"He repeated it to both of us in my room in the Commons. He told us quite clearly that we were not going to approve of some of the things the Government was going to do but that we would see it was going to immensely strengthen the Union and make it impregnable for all time." Molyneaux protested that this did not make sense, pointing out that if the Unionists were not going to like what was to appear then how was it going to strengthen the Union. Tebbit replied that the Government hoped to get the Dublin Government to remove its territorial claim over Northern Ireland and by doing so, the Union would be safe for all time.

Molyneaux, realistically, noted that considering the desire for eventual Irish unity amongst Dublin politicians, no political leader, however strong, could possibly risk such daring. However he still believes one report which has since been brought to his attention and which involved the ad hoc committee. FitzGerald had already stated that a referendum on divorce would be held during 1986 as part of his Constitutional Crusade. If this was approved then six months later a second would be held on Articles Two and Three of the Irish Constitution which lay claim over the North. This "secret" part of the Agreement obviously never came about after the failure of the divorce referendum and only after Garret FitzGerald resigned as Fine Gael leader in early 1987 did he admit that the rejection of the moderate divorce laws had been a bitter blow to him.

"The Tebbit committee which was a drafting cabal reached deadlock with the joint negotiating committee the weekend before the signing of the Agreement. The drafting committee stayed with the remit that if there was to be no withdrawal of the claim over territory then there would be no agreement. My report suggested that it was at this delicate stage that the American President Ronald Reagan became involved. The Irish Prime Minister reported to him the offer he had made on holding a referendum and then Reagan advised Thatcher to go ahead and sign the agreement on that understanding. He would act as guarantor but could not be held to it if the divorce referendum failed. That was the unseen part of the whole operation."

Leaks on what was being discussed were coming thick and fast during the September and October before the signing. All Molyneaux and Paisley could do was lobby fellow back benchers but most of the negotiations were taking place during the Parliamentary recess. MPs wanted to switch off from their own troubles let alone think about Northern Ireland. The two men were speaking into a vacuum.

As their working party lived up to its name and toiled, the leaders had a second meeting with the Prime Minister on October 30 – less than a month before the signing. This time Tom King sat opposite Ian Paisley. More outspoken than Douglas Hurd, it obviously followed that the meeting was more lively and now and then there were raised voices between the two men. Both the Prime Minister and her Cabinet colleague were more positive. The Unionist leaders too felt more sure of their position, simply because of the fact that so many details of the accord had been released. Molyneaux again raised the question of joint courts and this time Thatcher appeared better briefed. According to the Ulster Unionist leader they were never given the brush off but there were no assurances either.

"There were no denials that anything was going to happen. It was simply 'well, we will listen to what you have got to say because we recognise that you represent the majority in Northern Ireland'."

They basically knew what was to come but could only sit and wait for it to happen. Molyneaux felt frustrated that both the Prime Minister and the Secretary of State did not seem willing to recognise the resentment they would generate even amongst moderate Unionists. He was also angry at the Whitehall advisers for while he believed they were "bad enough" he did not think they were "mad enough" to embark on something which he felt was so doomed to failure. He and Powell had several late night discussions mulling over what was to come. By now, thanks to the mounting leaks, they could piece together a rough draft of the agreement. But there was still an air of incredulity between them that members of the Cabinet would back the plan, knowing that it would throw Northern Ireland into confusion and unrest.

By November 5 Tom King was condemning the "wild rumours" of what was to come. Speaking to Belfast Rotarians he said he was determined that nothing in any agreement would obstruct ways in which more of the administration of the Province could be returned to local people on a basis that would command widespread acceptance. That then, he said, was the background against which the Government was talking to Dublin. To secure a firm commitment to Northern Ireland's place within the UK and a firm determination to achieve a system of administration in the Province which "respects and reflects" the tradition of both communities.

The next day Molyneaux spoke in the debate on the Queen's Speech. He again hit out at ill-thought out Government initiatives and said the latest example was the Anglo-Irish discussions. He warned that uncertainty would increase if the Government yielded to the pressure to "establish a structure to give any foreign nation a role in administering or governing Northern Ireland" then it would demolish any written or verbal assurance that the status of Northern Ireland would not be affected. He maintained it would be clear to anyone with any common sense that the act of setting up a structure, with a permanent secretariat, was a clear contradiction of all earlier assurances.

The next week began the countdown to the signing. In a speech in Brussels on November 8 the Irish Prime Minister said a united Ireland had to take second place in the short term to providing a "stable, peaceful society" for Protestants and Roman Catholics in Northern Ireland. The SDLP held its annual conference over the Armistice weekend. While conversations on the accord were numerous during the social moments of the gathering, John Hume made little reference to it in his leader's speech. He only emphasised that he did not expect an immediate solution from the Anglo-Irish talks. Instead, he said, there could only be a healing process.

By November 11 – four days before the signing – Tom King confirmed that there was still no agreement. He said he did not know whether there would be a deal and noted that important issues still had to be resolved. There was one story which took the pending agreement almost off the front page – Northern Ireland qualified for the World Cup in Mexico after the team drew with England at Wembley. The *News Letter* carried a story the next day noting "Almost half a million Ulster viewers, for a brief night, forgot about the gloom and the pending Anglo-Eire summit, as they cheered themselves hoarse in front of the television".

Molyneaux came home from London on the morning of November 15 and watched from his aircraft as the Prime Minister's VC10 taxied along the runway to RAF Aldergrove. Before going to Parliament Buildings at Stormont for the Unionists' alternative summit, he travelled to Hillsborough and stood with Paisley outside the castle. Surrounded by members of the working party and Parliamentary colleagues they immediately announced that they would, from now on, be boycotting Northern Ireland Ministers. A letter of protest did not go into the hands of Tom King but a civil servant. It stated: "This amounts to a derogation from British sovereignty, is wholly incompatible with Northern Ireland being part of the UK and flies in the face of your repeated assurance of Ulster's right to self-determination". After a hymn and a prayer they departed from Stormont. There, with the working party, they drafted a response to the Agreement as it had already been agreed that there should be a definitive Unionist reply rather than a variety of "off the cuff" comments.

Meanwhile inside the former Governor's residence, the Prime Minister dressed in red, white and blue, signed the accord with Dr FitzGerald in front of an international cast of media and press. The master of ceremonies was Mrs Thatcher's press secretary Bernard Ingham. The joint communique said the aim was to promote peace and stability and the reconciliation of the two traditions. A joint ministerial conference would be set up and backed by a permanent secretariat at

Maryfield in east Belfast not far from the Stormont estate. There were 13 Articles in the agreement with the first setting out the status of Northern Ireland and emphasising that there would be no change unless it was wished by the majority; the next three set out the framework and objectives of the intergovernmental conference while Articles five to ten set out its functions; while the final three laid down that either government could ask for a review and the creation of an Anglo-Irish inter-parliamentary body.

The Prime Minister said her Government would do "its level best to resolve differences" and more than once she emphasised that the Agreement involved no derogation of Northern Ireland sovereignty. She was a loyalist and a Unionist and would remain so and stressed that the accord had been entered into in good faith in order to defeat the men of violence.

The alternative summit, with its smaller press entourage, called on all members of the DUP and Ulster Unionist Party to withdraw from every post or position on boards and agencies set up to assist or advise Northern Ireland Ministers. Those who did not would be branded as collaborators. A joint statement said that at every level of public life Ministers were going to be shunned.

It also called on the Prime Minister to announce a referendum so the people of Northern Ireland could register their views. If she did not, the statement said, then the Unionist MPs would resign their seats. The two leaders reiterated their commitment to an internal solution to Northern Ireland's problems on a basis of mutual respect and that they wanted nothing but a friendly relationship with Dublin.

Jim Molyneaux eventually got home. Only then was he able to sit down and think of his own views on the agreement: "As an Ulster citizen I felt we had been grossly betrayed. The betrayers, meaning the Whitehall establishment, would go on and on regardless of which ever government was in power. Influences had been brought to bear on the Prime Minister to force her to yield on principle. There was a great feeling of bitterness on my part because even though I tried to divorce myself from what small sacrifices I might have made during war time, I could not help but remember dozens of close friends who had been killed, some by my side, and all of them from Northern Ireland. You said to yourself, 'well, this is the reward isn't it'? My feelings at that time were no different from the average pro-Union citizen in Northern Ireland".

The political side was different. He started to go through what had happened and what could be done to reverse it. He instinctively felt there were limitations on what the Unionist parties could do but that it was up to the two leaders to muster as much opposition as possible and to hold their line. He also had to contend with the thought that he had very little of a political future left: "It was not despair but it was an instinctive feeling that everything you had worked for and fought for had been thrown away". He toyed with the idea, rather than all 15 MPs resigning, that he would do it alone. As leader of the Ulster Unionist Party he would resign and not fight a by-election. He wanted to simply state that he could not remain in a job where principles were so easily abandoned.

But the rest of the Parliamentary team were determined that a mass resignation would, at least, show, in a democratic manner, the depth of opposition to the accord. It was one of the few gestures they could make. In the days before the signing, in spite of Northern Ireland already turning its commercial thoughts to Christmas, there was a sense of betrayal amongst most pro-Union people – even those who had previously taken an impartial view of the political situation. One professional man in Belfast telephoned the Foreign Office in London and asked what were they going to do with him considering he was now a "displaced person with no country!" The Agreement was the talk of everywhere, whether it was the chip shop or the pub.

The *News Letter*, not known for its reserve, described it in one headline as "Backlash", while its leader column portrayed the deal as the "most divisive and dangerous initiative in the history of Northern Ireland". It did indeed push the two communities further apart. So pronounced was the reaction that it made the Irish Foreign Minister Peter Barry issue a direct appeal of "trust me" to Unionists emphasising that Molyneaux and Paisley were "absolutely, tragically wrong".

With the debate raging across Northern Ireland, the Prime Minister rose to make her statement on the accord to the House of Commons on November 18. She simply repeated an outline of the Agreement and reiterated her belief that it shored up Northern Ireland's sovereignty. One Conservative back bencher asked her why she had abandoned her Unionist principles to which he received the curt reply that she had not.

But it was Upper Bann MP Harold McCusker whose question made a lasting impression, if not on the House of Commons then certainly on home consumers. McCusker noted: "I never knew what desolation felt like until I read this Agreement last Friday afternoon. Does the Prime Minister realise that, when she carried the Agreement through the House, she will have ensured that I shall carry to my grave with ignomy the sense of the injustice that I have done to my constituents down the years, when, in their darkest hours, I exhorted them to put their trust in this British House of Commons which, one day, would honour its fundamental obligation to them to treat them as equal British citizens".

He took up the theme on the following Wednesday when the House went into the second day of debate on the Agreement. In Unionist minds the anger was still uppermost, the mass rally had been held and it had paid off in the numbers game. But the vote in the House, in spite of such graphic opposition, was going to be a foregone conclusion.

"I stood outside Hillsborough, not waving a Union flag – I doubt whether I will wave one again – not singing hymns, saying prayers or protesting, but like a dog, and asked the Government to put in my hand the document which sold my birthright.

I stood in the cold outside the gates of Hillsborough Castle and waited for them to come out and give me the Agreement second-hand. I felt desolate because as I stood in the cold outside Hillsborough Castle everything that I held dear turned to ashes in my mouth. Even in my most pessimistic moments, reading the precise detail in the Irish Press on the Wednesday before, I never believed that the Agreement would deliver me, in the context that it has, into the hands of those who, for 15 years, have murdered personal friends, political associates and hundreds of my constituents."

McCusker spoke from the heart. However 24 hours earlier when the Agreement debate first began his party leader took a different approach. In many ways it reflected his character as the McCusker speech did his. Molyneaux has never worn his feelings on his sleeve. He inherited from his mother a great patience and a manner of never letting other people know exactly what he was thinking. He has always felt that part of his duties as a party leader has been to remain calm, even when there is a crisis going on around him. But he also likes to do the opposite to what the general perception of him is and so he decided to deliver his speech in a mood contrary to what the House expected.

"I decided that the Government members would be imagining that the Ulster Unionists would come ranting and raving, insulting everybody. This, of course, would have been an enormous help to the Government. Having concluded that that was exactly what they would want us to do, I then did the opposite. It was not a speech which was admired very much, even from within my own party. To many, maybe, it sounded a bit too weak but it was designed to put the Government on the spot."

He spoke of the responsibilities he had as a leader: "During my six years as leader of the Ulster Unionist Party, my objective has been to achieve for all the people of Northern Ireland those prizes of peace, stability and reconciliation. As leader of the largest party in Northern Ireland I feel, as I have always felt, that I have a duty to lead. For any party leader, that means some political risk. I accepted those risks, because I had to consider – today I still have to consider – the young people to whom the Prime Minister referred when she spoke at Hillsborough on the day of the signing. The fact that I am nearer the finishing post than are those young people, makes that consideration all the more compelling".

Molyneaux cited the example of three young people – Catholics – who had attended the City Hall rally: "They begged me to persuade the Prime Minister to think again and, as one of them put it to 'beg her not to condemn us to spending the rest of our lives in an atmosphere of distrust and tension with our Protestant neighbours'. That was a very moving occasion for me.

That grim prospect has been publicly recognised by church representatives, authoritative newspaper editors, moderate organisations and individuals, and, most of all, by those who have worked so hard for reconciliation in Northern Ireland and are now depressed because all that they have achieved has been obliterated at a stroke".

He ended by referring to the Prime Minister, pointing out that she had, over the years, asked him about attitudes in Northern Ireland: "In what may be my last contribution in the House, I am sure she will not object if I report to her in the presence of Rt hon. and hon. members, I have to say honestly and truthfully that in 40 years in public life I have never known what I can only describe as a universal cold fury, which some of us have thus far managed to contain. I beg the Prime Minister not to misjudge the situation but to examine and assess the damage which will be done to the aims of peace, stability and reconciliation. Perhaps the leader of the Labour Party and the leaders of the other opposition parties will not mind me saying to the Prime Minister that she will lose nothing in the eyes of the House or of the country if she decides to steer a safer course". She sat opposite him and stared straight ahead, expressionless.

It was the last speech he was to make in the House for almost two years. Parliament overwhelmingly endorsed the Agreement with a vote of 473 to 47 and the accord "entered into force" on Friday November 29 when the formal notification of acceptance was exchanged between the two governments.

As set out at the City Hall rally in a "solemn oath", the two leaders began organising the mass resignations. They had set themselves the deadline of January 1, 1986, so it took all of Molyneaux's Parliamentary "behind the scenes skills" to ensure that they were effective and the scheme worked.

While Tom King faced physical abuse in Belfast city centre and his Ministers were hounded by flag waving loyalists across the land, Molyneaux set about organising and putting into motion the Westminster wheels which allowed all 15 men to resign together. However throughout the protest, Molyneaux kept reminding colleagues and party officers that such a move would not make the Government change its stated policy. He saw it as a marker which might impress other MPs but have little further effect. He was horrified to learn that there were those within both Unionist parties who believed such a "mini referendum" would change the Government's attitude overnight. This, as far as he was concerned, was not living up to the real world of politics.

In spite of his recognised enjoyment of Parliament and its procedures which suited his methodical mind, the idea of resigning did not annoy him. He had already thought of doing a "solo operation" and not returning at all to the London political arena so the resignation protest seemed the proper course to take: "It made sense to me. At the time of crisis in Northern Ireland it was a bit of a nonsense for us to be sitting in the House of Commons listening to a debate which had no bearing on the lives of our constituents who were facing a period of upheaval".

He also backed the Parliamentary boycott in the wake of the elections which were held on January 23, 1986. Unlike Powell who felt he had to remain in the House, Molyneaux believed there was no point in being at Westminster and giving credibility to the Parliament which had approved the Agreement. There was, according to the Ulster Unionist leader, no friction between Powell and himself over the South Down member's decision to remain although it created uncertainty and criticism among party rank and file.

"I recognised that Enoch was a Parliamentarian who felt that if he was earning a salary then he had to be in the House. Whereas I was there two, maybe three, days a week keeping the machinery going but I felt it was wrong to go into the Chamber or the division lobby."

The writs for the 15 by-elections were moved on December 17 by leading Conservative back bencher Sir Peter Emery. The Unionists had forced them through the procedure of having taken up offices "of profit under the Crown". Molyneaux, along with several others, had accepted a stewardship in Three Chiltern Hundreds of Stoke, Desborough and Burnham in Buckinghamshire while the others took up the non-existent post in Northstead. To ensure too that each seat was contested the two parties had to put up a token candidate "Peter Barry" in four constituencies. The January by-elections, in spite of the winter weather, saw 481,330 people vote in protest against the Agreement. The Unionist share of the total poll was 71.5 per cent as compared with 62.3 per cent in the 1983 General Election and Molyneaux had a majority of 29,186.

But the Unionists lost the Newry/Armagh seat to SDLP deputy leader Seamus Mallon. Molyneaux had recognised the risk as had the sitting MP Jim Nicholson. He warned party members that even if a record number of people voted against the Agreement, Nicholson losing the seat would be the focus of media attention. This dutifully happened.

The 14 re-elected Unionists had shown, by orchestrating their own referendum, that the majority of people in Northern Ireland were against the Agreement. But Molyneaux knew that while it was a milestone and would be remembered in Parliament, the opposition band wagon was only the first few hundred yards down the long, hard road he warned of the previous November.

He left the platform that day realising that while his speech had not suited some of his colleagues, he had set down the reality of the situation and had not built up false hopes. In his quiet, calm manner he knew that the Agreement would not be destroyed overnight. His views as to why he delivered such a dogmatic message to such a massive crowd sum up, in many ways, his own character.

"If I had stood up and said 'This day marks the end of the Agreement, you can take it that as from next Monday it is wiped out, there will be no need for the Parliamentary debate' then that would have been highly irresponsible and highly damaging to morale. It would have meant that people would have sat all weekend waiting to hear the announcement that it was all over. They had to be told that it was just the beginning of a long, hard haul. That message had to be got across. I suppose they may have wanted to hear 'By the numbers that are here today, this spells the end of the Anglo-Irish Agreement, go out tonight and celebrate'. That might have got more cheers but it would not have been fair to them." If anything, Molyneaux has always been a realist.

2.   War

On the morning prior to the Assembly elections of October 20, 1982, an incendiary device was planted on a window sill outside the Ulster Unionist headquarters in Belfast's Glengall Street.

In the room directly behind the bomb stood Jim Molyneaux and the South Belfast MP the Rev Martin Smyth. They were looking at a string of leaflets for different constituencies, spread out on a large wooden table. These were to be dropped in a last minute election blitz before voters went to the poll the next day.

The then party secretary Norman Hutton entered the room and in a matter of fact way, suggested it would be prudent if the two men moved upstairs as a gift had been left on the window sill outside.

Molyneaux recalls the incident: "We looked around and there it was in our full view. Two petrol cans attached to a lunch box in between. And I remember, it is one of those funny things which you do in that type of situation, I said to Martin, 'you bring that lot and I'll lift this bundle'. Not content with that Martin went back for some posters which he needed and we strolled upstairs".

There was a similar attitude among the staff upstairs in the general office which was right over the bomb. One secretary did not want to move at all, complaining that if the device went off leaflets and letters would be strewn across the street and hard work would have literally gone out the window.

Molyneaux eventually ushered everyone into a back room, amid the grumbles of work being disrupted. An Army bomb disposal team had already been called and the staff realised it would be hours before normality reigned again.

They had been instructed by the RUC that no one should leave the building but the Ulster Unionist leader had already planned three separate visits to canvassing teams across the country. Norman Hutton was asked to quickly open the gates to the office car park and Molyneaux, already in his vehicle, darted out, turned right and drove towards the famous Boyne Bridge.

But when he got there a Land Rover was slewed across the road, preventing traffic from driving down into Glengall Street. There was a gap on the left hand side between the vehicle and a concrete rubbish bin which sat at the corner of the road.

Molyneaux takes up the story: "I thought to myself, well there is not much room but try and avoid the Land Rover as if I scrape the car against the litter bin I will only damage my own car and there won't be an inquiry".

He managed to squeeze through – just – and thought nothing more of the incident until he switched on the car radio to hear what the latest situation was at headquarters.

But what he heard instead was an announcer calmly stating that the nearby Sandy Row was now also sealed off after the discovery of a second device planted in a concrete rubbish bin at the top of Glengall Street. He laughs while recalling this and only notes that he realises he should have been more alert.

More was to come. He was up early on election morning, had voted and had begun a tour of the polling stations in his South Antrim constituency. By the time he had reached Lisburn about an hour and a half later he kept receiving messages to telephone home at Aldergrove immediately.

There was no reply and at the next station he was informed that he had to ring the police at Antrim. When he eventually got through he was told there was a bomb at his sister-in-law Agnes' home, the family farm, and could he get back swiftly.

Molyneaux's response, after inquiring if the family was safe, was by asking what on earth could he do. He finished the Lisburn tour and returned to Aldergrove to witness the Army bomb disposal team at work. It was another incendiary device and the second he had driven past within 24 hours.

"It was again placed on the window sill but I did not see it because when I went out that morning I had swerved to the right and so could not see that part of the house. Indeed Agnes did not notice it until she went into the front room and saw it sitting outside."

Molyneaux still had no realisation that he was a terrorist target but from that morning he has had to live with a security presence – day and night. The failed IRA attack eventually came home to him a few weeks later when he again had to suppress laughter.

"It was on that day that I lost my feedom of movement. A few weeks after the election I asked a senior RUC officer when would it end and why was it continuing. Afterall, the election was over and all the fuss had died down. But what he said to me was 'what you do not realise, and somebody higher up must have put this into his head, is that if the Assembly works and we have a government of some kind, you will stand a fair chance of being Prime Minister – that is why you have to put up with this sort of thing'. At that point I rather irreverently laughed and still do."

This was not Jim Molyneaux being derisory of the policeman or of his views. Nor was he being blasé about the attempted attack on the family home.

Through active service during the Second World War he saw the aftermath in the relief of Belsen which was completely beyond comprehension. Experiences like that do leave their mark. It made him wonder how one human being could inflict such pain on another and a niggling worry that it could happen again.

War also left him with a sense that you had to contribute something to life and not take it immediately for granted. As he notes himself, in active service a man put his life consciously into a pool and if he was lucky it came back to him.

Through that sort of training when emotions could not be shown when dreadful events were taking place, Molyneaux has applied to all aspects of his life ever since. That was why there was no fuss or loud mouthed condemnation about the attacks on his party's headquarters or on his family home.

It was natural that he should join the "Brylcreem Boys". The present RAF Aldergrove stands on Molyneaux land and as an adolescent he watched one squadron leader go on his meteorological flight in his biplane from Aldergrove out over Donegal to the Atlantic. It was a daily occurrence and one which fascinated Molyneaux who could set his watch by the perfect timing of the operation.

James Henry Molyneaux was the eldest son of William and Cissie. His first influence was another James Henry – his paternal grandfather. He lived on the family's other farm at Seacash and when his eldest grandson called in he would discuss the national and international events of the day. He took *The Times* and *The Daily Telegraph* and would have read them over breakfast.

The older man treated James Henry as an equal in terms of age. He never patted him on the head and spoke child's talk and he always gave him both his names.

"He would not take account of me being, say a boy of 12. Instead he would have said to me as you would to a grown-up – 'well James Henry, I do not like the way they are handling the balance of payments or Britain going off the Gold Standard. It is all a very serious matter'. I, of course, did not know about these things at all but as soon as I enquired about them I would receive an explanation which I could immediately grasp. He would also read out to me quotes from the Prime Minister of the day and in a curious way I became much more interested in the national and international politics rather than what was going on in Northern Ireland."

After public elementary, James Henry, being the eldest son, went immediately onto the farm. His first prized possession was an incubator for 150 eggs. As he notes: "I thought I was going to produce miracles and then we purchased hatching eggs and I concentrated on the poultry end. I bought more incubators and the business went fairly well. In between organising this I helped on the farm".

However this changed as war loomed. There was a shortage of horses and carts to build the Aldergrove aerodrome and it was the done thing for each farmer in the area to put on at least one horse and cart, especially adapted with rubber tyres – the first James Henry had ever seen.

The young man remained with this work until he joined up in 1941. He had always wanted to do it but had found it difficult to find an excuse until the Blitz on Belfast during April and May of that year.

His parents who understandably did not want to lose their 20-year-old eldest son, could not refuse any longer.

"I had made up my mind privately to do it but after the Blitz I had something to strengthen my hand. The parents, like good parents, were reluctant to encourage me. But after the bombing of Belfast everyone started to take the war much more seriously and I found myself joining up with many of my mates."

James Henry joined up in Belfast and became Aircraftman Molyneaux – the lowest of the low, according to himself. He went to Liverpool and then to Padgate which was the intake station and then to Wimslow for initial training. His first posting was to Dyce which is now Aberdeen's airport where he stayed for 18 months before starting southwards.

Looking back on it now he sees that there was something symbolic in the movement as he travelled down the east coast of Britain until he got to Tangmere which was a sector station for 11th Group Fighter Command which, in turn, became the epicentre of the tactical airforce which spearheaded the "D" Day invasion plans.

The young man clad now in khaki battledress, decided matter-of-factly that it was a foregone conclusion that he would be "over there" at an early stage of the massive invasion.

"D" Day was to take place on June 5, 1944. Molyneaux in his small unit under Wing Commander Reggie Gould was loaded at Tilbury on the Saturday night before. The aircraftman saw his posting to wing headquarters under Gould as "good fortune". His commanding officer had been a pilot during the First War and was an impressive character. He had stood as a Conservative candidate in Shropshire and early in the posting he struck a chord with Molyneaux who readily admits that he was already a Conservative with a small "c".

He had been an admirer of Anthony Eden, probably with some of his grandfather's influence, and had found it easy to identify with him – particularly after Neville Chamberlain sacked him from his Cabinet for wanting the Government to take firmer action against the rise of Fascism.

Small incidents during an overall event always seem to be remembered better than the actual happening. So it was at Tilbury.

"It is the funny, insignificant things which always get you. We were standing in a three tonner with youngsters standing outside the perimeter wire waving to us, knowing perfectly well where we were going. Suddenly the boys started digging into their pockets for coins, instantly throwing them out and the children scrambling for them. We knew then that we might never need British currency again."

Molyneaux's small wing headquarters unit of about nine men, along with hundreds of others, were towed and then anchored in the Thames estuary far below Tilbury waiting for the "off" signal.

Another of his remembrances was the hymn singing on the ships on the Sunday morning. All the services began at 11.00 am and the sound travelled from ship to ship across the water. Whereas Molyneaux recollects the begrudged attendance for parade service, the service that morning held much more meaning.

"There was much more feeling and a reality to it because most of them knew what was in store for them."

They were due to move out on the Sunday night but the invasion was postponed by Eisenhower for 24 hours because of a ferocious storm in the English Channel.

However at 4.00 am on June 5 the omens changed and the Supreme Commander of Allied Forces in Europe took the step which put 156,000 Allied troops in France by nightfall on the following day.

Molyneaux's ship, like all the rest, was marshalled into two lines of a convoy. He describes it as a spectacle as, to him, it was fascinating to watch, see how it all worked and try to understand the planning involved. At this stage everything was going like clockwork.

The first, stark glimpse of what war truly meant came as the convoy got to the Straits of Dover where the two lines of ships were merging into one. The German guns across the Channel had already picked up the convoy on radar and had begun shelling.

At this stage Molyneaux and his friends thought the situation was exciting and stood watching as the shells missed the ships and showered their decks with water. However this initial burst of enthusiasm was soon dampened when a shell hit the ship ahead.

"It was a ship with a mixture of cargo on board with light skinned vehicles on the top, tanks and ammunition below. The shell hit the top lorries. Then the whole thing went ablaze and the burning petrol caught the ammunition and she actually disintegrated in a huge mushroom of cloud. Bits of the ship and bodies all raining down on us. However we got through that ordeal and got to the Isle of Wight which had become known as Piccadilly Circus."

What was more memorable for Molyneaux than arriving at this "roundabout" was that when they had got on board Wing Commander Gould had briefed his small unit of nine men. He told them he did not know exactly where they were going but that he had a sealed package and he pointed out where it was in case anything happened.

They were all informed that whoever survived had to get the package but not open it until they were outside a three mile limit of territorial waters. It was only after they had gone south of the Isle of Wight did the Wing Commander open the package and discover where they were going – Normandy. There was also a marking on a map of an exact location where the small unit was to establish an airfield.

"We were not going to capture an existing one. What we had to do was find the place, decide if it was suitable, bring in the airfield construction team, set up the anti-aircraft squadron all around to protect it and then, hopefully, get the Spitfires in within 24 hours."

The instructions seemed straightforward on paper but the unit did not achieve its goal for more than four days as the Germans were entrenched on the site. Instead, they made a secondary strip at a small place called Beny sur Mer.

"Eventually we did achieve the target. Once we got the construction underway we actually had three squadrons of Spitfires who did their sorties and then landed on our new airstrip. It was pretty good going, but I had a very small part in it."

Molyneaux admits that when he first joined up it was a shock to the system in having to suppress his individuality. Aircraftmen, like himself, were told in no uncertain terms that they were not allowed to think – it was being done for them by somebody else. But he describes it as "fateful" that he was posted to Wing Commander Gould at wing headquarters.

"You suddenly became an indispensable cog in something more attractive to my rather devious and inquiring mind. We all knew as much as the Wing Commander – we had to because of the danger if he became a casualty anyone of us had to be able to take over out of necessity wherever it might be."

This actually happened on one occasion when Molyneaux was left as the acting Wing Commander – but still only ranking as a leading aircraftman.

His unit was south of the Rhine at a small airfield at Grave during the famous Operation Market Garden which included the battle for Arnhem, now immortalised in the film "A Bridge Too Far".

They had a very heavy attack by the Messerschmitt 262 jet bombers – the first time they had been seen over the British Second Army area which had established itself on a line from Zwolle through Deventer up to Arnhem. The bombers peppered the small airfield with anti-personnel bombs which contained shrapnel – deadly to both the men and the grounded aircraft.

"We were pretty well plastered that night and we had our wing operation room actually in the morgue attached to a Roman Catholic church in the village. I was sitting there manning the headquarters and my immediate job was to ring the three squadron commanders, all of whom were squadron leaders, to ask them their state of readiness, how many casualties they had and aircraft damaged.

"I was trying to do it in a civil sort of way and most of them understood. The reason for my action was that 83 Group headquarters had to know immediately in case they had to get reserve aircraft and men out from England."

But there was one squadron leader who did not approve of being addressed by the "lowest of the low" in the ranks. He became agitated by Molyneaux's persistent questions.

"He inquired who I was and when I told him he replied 'how dare you pester me with such a fiddling inquiry in the aftermath of battle with my men dead and injured'. I said I did appreciate his situation but I explained it was my job to get back such information to group headquarters and that it had to come through our office so it could be co-ordinated.

"He lost his temper completely and I said well, I am sorry but I have no option but to tell the group commander that you have refused to co-operate. I was told to go to hell with a few other expletives. I could understand it as he was new to the whole scene.

"When I did report to the operations officer at headquarters and gave the information I was asked what the story was with the third squadron. I had to tell him that the officer had refused to give it to me on the grounds that I was not sufficiently senior."

Molyneaux's wing commander on a couple of occasions had suggested to him that he would put him forward for a commission. This was refused by the aircraftman on the grounds that to gain it he would have had to have returned to a desk job in England. He said "thank you but no", and prefered to stay where he was. As for the rude squadron leader – he was disciplined and reduced in rank over the incident.

He believes there is an exact parallel between this experience and the world of politics. From being an ordinary rank and file member in a squadron of 200 he was placed in a key position where he knew everything that was going on within the entire operation of the Second Army and 83 Group of the tactical air force.

Exactly the same happened to him in politics. For four years he was a mere back bencher in the Conservative and Unionist Party. There a member was told nothing and if he asked he was told to mind his own business.

"Even today it is true to say that the back benchers of the two main parties who do not participate in decision making are just simply guided by the duty whip standing at the lobby door and giving them the thumb 'in there boy'. If they stop to ask what they are voting for, they are told to keep moving and stop blocking the entrance. It is as bad as that.

"The parallel between politics and the war happened when Ted Heath refused to offer us the whip in 1974 after the February election and we were forced to create our own grouping at Westminster. Then six months later I became leader of the Unionist coalition as well as already being leader of the Ulster Unionist members. You were suddenly into a re-run of that war time experience where you got to know things and you had to know them, not because they wanted you to, but if you did not then you would gum up the works."

He readily admits that he would not have missed his work at wing headquarters for anything. It made, he says, all the previous foot slogging worthwhile.

After the creation of another larger airfield at the Dutch village of Helmond, east of Eindhoven, the unit waited until the Allied Forces crossed the Rhine in March the following year. It was dreaded – particularly with the defeat at Arnhem still fresh in everyone's minds.

"Thankfully the disaster did not happen as the German Army simply had cracked. We, however, did not know this and feared the Rhine crossing more than Normandy as we had already seen what could go wrong."

From there they moved to Hanover and then to Luneburg which was near Belsen concentration camp. Molyneaux's unit arrived three days after it had been liberated by the Second Army.

"The British Army field hospitals concentrated all their resources on doing what they could for the poor devils. They were getting it so tight that they asked if the mobile RAF hospital could be moved up to help them. It was our unit which escorted it up to the camp. It was a pretty harrowing experience. It was worse than anyone could ever have imagined. Unless you had seen it with your own eyes you would not have believed the suffering and you certainly would not want anyone else to see it."

As at other events, it is the small things which he remembers most: "A very simple thing was that you were handed a roll of insulating tape which you used to silence the horn of the jeep so that you would not, by accident, sound it. This was because driving slowly through the camp, there were bodies lying all over the place around which you had to swerve but there were also all the poor people who were staggering along these roads in some sort of coma. It was not unknown, at the beginning, that when the drivers sounded their horns to make them gently get out of the way for their own safety that they just dropped dead with the shock".

He also remembers being prepared for the camp before the mobile hospital was moved up to help in the relief work: "We all had to go and get inoculated and dusted from head to foot with a powder which was supposed to protect us from lice and other insects. The place was hiving with them and there was a great worry that Typhus would spread".

Molyneaux's first reaction was one of complete and utter disbelief. While he had read about the atrocities and had seen some pictures, he still kept asking himself if they were being published for propaganda purposes. The size of the place also came as a shock to him – thousands of people crumpled together dying.

"There was just this overwhelming feeling of disbelief that any human being could do that kind of thing to other human beings."

Rage also rose when the SS officers from the camp who were forced to carry out relief work and dig mass graves, still continued to ill-treat the internees. If one was about to collapse in front of an officer he simply booted that prisoner in the face.

"Then I am afraid the Geneva Convention went out the window and the boys just got stuck into the Germans." He too became involved on a couple of occasions: "It was very difficult to restrain yourself when you had able bodied SS men continuing to ill-treat, in your presence, their victims who were on the point of death".

From then on he was always conscious of what had happened and had nightmares in the post-war years: "It was always conscious, you were always conscious of it. You thought a lot about it and you thought could it all happen again if things get out of hand. Of course it was compounded by other wartime atrocities."

Molyneaux does not believe that ex-servicemen are any better than their civilian contemporaries but he does think that after witnessing the death of friends standing beside them, they do carry a sense of responsibility.

"It is not high-faluting. It is an awareness of how precious life is and that you must not fritter it away. It makes you take life more seriously because you have a kind of feeling that, after every battle, you have been given your life back. The reasons being that you have, to some extent, put your life consciously into a pool and if your are lucky you will get it back."

The loss of friends has also had a bearing on the way Molyneaux has shaped his character ever since. He was left feeling that you could never depend on human beings not to carry out the same torture on others.

As usual, he points out that many others went through the same experience of witnessing the deaths of their friends in action.

"You do not feel thereafter that you have a right to lead your own life. I am not saying this is a high minded way but you do develop a kind of conscience and that you cannot come home and be selfish. You cannot say I am going to enjoy myself now because you have an unspoken kind of a thought that you have to do your dead mate's job as well as your own." It is why he derives more satisfaction out of sorting out a person's mobility allowance than speaking in the House of Commons.

His first loss of friends was during an air raid on the beachhead shortly after his unit had landed in Normandy. The second was during the battle to capture Caen when the command headquarters and its squadrons were sited in an orchard beside a Canadian regiment. He had first got to know some of the men when they waiting for a week in compounds to load up at Tilbury.

"They used to tease me about the Irish not knowing the taste of peanut butter and they would feed me on it and what white loaf they had. We managed to reunite on the beachhead which wasn't too difficult considering that everyone was cramped together.

"They were an infantry division and had to go into action. The horrifying part was that the casualties were brought back to that orchard. You were not being ghoulish but you would go over to see who the casualties were.

"There you would discover them just lying there wrapped in blankets with their identity discs pinned to the top of them. The Royal Engineers dug the graves in a paddock which adjoined our orchard and theirs and I remember going over with the Army chaplain for the burials, as there were no such things as funerals as we know them. Suddenly you were standing there looking at them, the blankets just sown up, no coffins, and their bare feet sticking out the bottom. It did make a mark on you when you thought that you had been laughing and joking with them the night before."

Since then he has felt he has had to pay back for surviving: "Because you do think about the half dozen of friends who did not come back and you have the sort of feeling that why were they taken, why was it not me. It is just something of which you are conscious".

There was a brief interlude after the relief of Belsen when the April ceasefire began to take effect.

This was vividly brought home to Molyneaux at Luneburg when he went for a walk around the base to the control tower. The place was deserted except for one controller and there was a deadly hush all over the airfield. The aircraftman asked what was up and received the simple reply "nothing to do". All the planes were grounded from the Typhoons to the Meteors and for the first time Molyneaux began to think that maybe the war was really coming to an end.

However Wing Commander Gould had other ideas. The next mission for his small unit was to secure an airfield at Flemsburg in Schleswig-Holstein where the Germans had brought their experimental jets fearing they would fall into the Russians' hands. The Air Officer commanding 83 Group – one Harry Broadhurst – wanted to ensure that the Germans did not destroy them.

So Reggie Gould transformed his unit into a mobile column and they pushed through the Second Army towards Lubeck and the Kiel Canal. This was still under the authority of the German Navy with its men protecting the bridge over the famous waterway. Molyneaux was driving the armoured car on top of which was perched the Wing Commander. He, in turn, was having an argument with a German officer, covered by heavy machine guns, who was refusing to give right of way.

The aircraftman takes up the story: "I tugged at the Wing Commander's ankle and he looked down and demanded to know what the hell was it now. In reply I suggested that he inform the officer that we were going to see Admiral Karl Donitz. So in a mixture of German and English he gave him the message adding 'get that bloody barrier up out of the way'. His sheer weight of personality got us through and the sailors all saluted.

He then sat down beside me and asked 'what had put the idea of Donitz into your head'. So I admitted that I had a confession to make and told him that while I had been listening on the radio for instructions I had tuned into the forces broadcasting station and suddenly it came through that Hitler had committed suicide and had handed over to Donitz as the German Commander in Chief. The German naval officer must have known that he was in Schleswig-Holstein and that I had not had time to inform the Wing Commander. He replied that it was a 'bloody good job' I had told him when I did or 'we probably would all have been shot'."

The small column arrived at the airfield which was overflowing with German Luftwaffe, including their lady friends. They had fled the Russian front and had come back to the relative safety of Schleswig-Holstein.

Here again it is the small incident which remains in his mind: "It was quite incredible. Two Junkers' 88's landed as we were negotiating with the station's commandant and the planes taxied towards the airstrip's apron. The bomb doors opened and all these bundles fell onto the concrete. With that the bundles got up and ran. They turned out to be German airmen who had been packed into the fuselage – they had actually been in the bomb racks. Obviously they must have hung on until the bomb doors were closed and then lowered themselves down until the plane had landed. Then they had to lift themselves up again until the doors opened. It was most extraordinary. They were simply so scared of the Russians and were fleeing back from airfields which had been overrun".

The handover of the station went smoothly with the Wing Commander demanding accommodation for his men – in spite of the overcrowding and the female entourage. As these negotiations continued there was an almighty explosion outside and the remains of one of the experimental jets lay on the tarmac.

After surveying the damage Molyneaux drove Reggie Gould back to the commandant: "The Wing Commander kicked open the door, drew his revolver and shouted 'You have cheated me, you have cheated me commandant' who promptly gave the usual Hitler salute. The Wing Commander then said 'and don't bloody salute like that or I will shoot you on the spot. I am warning you and it is the last warning, if any more of those jets are blown up I shall come down here personally and execute you and nine of your officers'. So that put an end to that nonsense. We got out jets safeguarded until the reinforcements arrived up and we were able to put proper guards on them".

The airfield was secured and then came what Molyneaux describes as the painful process of disarming the Luftwaffe officers who still carried their personal weapons. So scared were they of the Russians that they wanted to keep their pistols to defend their families and themselves as they believed the Allied Forces would leave them to their fate.

"I remember we were standing beside the commandant, watching all the young officers taking out revolvers from their holsters, handing them to their adjutant who just threw them on a heap of weapons. This young man came forward of good bearing but not haughty, with tears rolling down his face. Instead of handing over the revolver, he pulled it out as if he was going to use it on our Wing Commander. With that the adjutant grabbed his wrist and flung the revolver to the ground. He was taken away under close arrest but the Wing Commander did send a note to the commandant asking that no further discipline be taken against him. I will always remember the fear on their faces – simply because they did not want to be taken by the Russians."

The whole process at Flemsburg took several weeks and by then the Allied Military Government began to take control. The authorities decided that the only way they could feed and organise the defeated German nation was to use the existing leadership at local level. This went against the grain for many, including Molyneaux, who compares it with having to work with Sinn Fein in Northern Ireland's council chambers. There was no time to give them security clearance – so no one knew who had been a Nazi and who had not. The authorities simply had to use them because they had the organisational power to do things.

"It went hard with us as it sometimes goes hard with us nowadays when you see people who are in line with violence – Sinn Fein – and you have to sit in councils and work with them. It was the same feeling then."

After a week or two of this restoration of some local administration, Molyneaux was able to see politics emerging again.

"The first sign of this was that we had to withdraw from certain areas. Most of our boys were horrified because they could not see, after having won territory at the expense of lives, why they were being told to leave. What they did not know and I suppose it is something I should not have known, was that in our little headquarters we had a copy of the Yalta Agreement plans for the dismemberment of Germany and its demarcation lines. I could see – even while the war was still on – that from these maps we could go so far and if we advanced further then, eventually, we would have to withdraw. I remember being quite clear about it and saying to myself well, why are we going over there because we are not going to be allowed to keep that. That was the start of the politiking."

The problem of feeding and finding accommodation for the population was immense – particularly as it was expected to be completed before winter set in. The administrative side of this operation was quite staggering and Molyneaux was able to see it from the inside.

"It was, I suppose, good training because you were studying what had been a fairly efficient type of local administration. It was a good education because I noticed when I became a county councillor in the early 1960's that suddenly part of all of that fell into place. A councillor coming in from a rural area found it difficult to understand the allocation of resources. For example, if he saw a road needed to be fixed, he would question why the job could not be carried out as it only needed a small amount of tar to do so. You would not instinctively take the side of the bureaucrats but you would be instinctively thinking well, now, how many cubic yards of tar macadam is it going to take to fix that road and how many roads in similar disrepair do we have in County Antrim and how are we going to ensure that they are all repaired. So I suppose the war experience did help."

His involvement with the administration of the Military Government went side by side with another consideration – the war in the Far East was still going on. Both he and his Wing Commander volunteered to go and they got as far as the preliminary interviews. Reggie Gould had already admitted that he was probably too old but that Molyneaux had a good chance being young and single. But that all ended with the dropping of the atomic bomb on Hiroshima on August 6, 1945.

Molyneaux had had the choice of either going to the Far East, being demobilised when his turn came, or taking a peacetime commission in the RAF – something Gould would have backed him on.

"But when I started to think of the way things were changing even then, you were getting back to the spit and polish type of routine – simply because you had nothing else to do, you had no aircraft to keep in the air, you had no airfields to defend, your anti-aircraft squadrons were not needed. There was nothing for it but to keep the troops occupied with endless parades, inspections and route marches. So after what had been valuable work you were suddenly faced with an absolutely meaningless exercise. It was one of the influences which made me rule out the peacetime regular Air Force."

The accumulative affect of his experiences during the war has had a bearing on his character ever since. Always understated but always there. He has been severely criticised from both within his party since he became leader and from outside, over his apparent lack of emotion – so evident in other Ulster politicians. But his personal make-up simply will not allow him to fall into that stereotyped role.

Top ranking members of his own party have accused him of being a cold-hearted bastard but they forget that he has witnessed much worse scenes of man's inhumanity to man than to go "over the top" on the latest disturbance in what has become the gold fish bowl of Northern Ireland politics.

It is not that he does not care but as he points out himself, if you show signs of fear then it will be distributed amongst others and signs of such emotion help no one. He was never a war hero but he saw enough to be taught that you do not over-react to situations which are beyond your control.

This can be seen in the way he has taken on the responsibility of calming others when a certain situation, particularly in Northern Ireland, could get out of hand.

It was Jim Molyneaux who had to hold in his own emotions and, at the same time, reassure others during the aftermaths of the murders of Robert Bradford and Edgar Graham both, in their own way, leading and influential members of the Glengall Street party. It also had an influence on his reaction to the murder of Airey Neave by the INLA at the House of Commons in March 1979.

Airey Neave was both Shadow Northern Ireland Secretary and head of Margaret Thatcher's private office – a powerful position. The value to the Unionist MPs was that when they had had discussions with Neave about Northern Ireland matters, they knew that he could also get a message immediately to Mrs Thatcher if he felt it necessary.

Molyneaux and he worked closely together, obviously because of this link, but also because there was a sound friendship between the two men and they got on well together. Both had had varied experiences during the war, never stuck in the one place, and they could talk about security in a similar language.

He remembers joking with Neave in the Commons tea room the day before he was blown up in a bomb planted under his car within the precincts of Parliament. The Labour Government had just been defeated in a censure motion and the talk at Westminster was full of the forthcoming General Election. Neave, with Molyneaux's help, had drawn up the Northern Ireland section of the Conservative manifesto which included the establishment of administrative devolution in the Province.

"I remember saying to him 'you are going to have to divide your mental concentration as there is a bit of light reading being prepared for you'. He said something along the lines of 'oh, you mean the Northern Ireland Office' and I nodded my head. He said he had heard it too and I pointed out that it was going to be a massive brief which was designed to turn him away from what was to appear in the manifesto. He and I obviously knew what the other was thinking and what was going to be in the document. Airey said that his version tallied with my own but he emphasised 'they will have some job turning us'. By that he meant himself and Mrs Thatcher."

He was dead within 24 hours and Molyneaux believes it had a devastating affect on Conservative policy towards Northern Ireland. Administrative devolution never came about and instead the Secretary of State in the Conservative administration Humphrey Atkins called his round table conference which Molyneaux refused to attend.

He was deeply upset by Neave's murder, did not show it, but has continually pointed out ever since to leading Conservatives as well as Mrs Thatcher herself that they did a U-turn on their 1979 election manifesto.

The murder of Robert Bradford by the IRA at his South Belfast constituency surgery in Finaghy on November 15, 1981, was even closer in terms of loss and the effect it had on the Ulster Unionist Party.

"I remember meeting him as a young minister and he was one of the sort who would have had a short discussion with you and then, at the end of it, say I found that interesting could we arrange a meeting and discuss it further sometime," Molyneaux recalls.

Bradford stood as a Vanguard Unionist in the anti-Sunningdale General Election in February 1974 against Faulkner Unionist Rafton Pounder and beat him by a majority of more than 3,000.

It was natural that when the 11 United Ulster Unionist Council members returned to Westminster that the fledglings like Robert Bradford, Harold McCusker and Willie Ross sought out the experience of the "old stager" Molyneaux while the "big three" of Ian Paisley, Harry West and Bill Craig divided their time between London and the Province.

One of the first things which struck Molyneaux who, by this stage was the coalition's secretary and whip at Westminster, was Robert Bradford's quick mind.

"He had a very fertile brain and was always doing what is necessary and essential in any political party. He was always producing original ideas to spark off constructive discussion. He would never accept that just because something looked a certain way on the surface that that was the way it had to be."

Molyneaux also noticed through the years that because of Bradford's clerical background in the Methodist Church (which he resigned from in 1974) that he tended to take a moral viewpoint on many political issues without wearing his Christianity on his sleeve.

"He was a very sincere Christian but he was never judgemental about the rest of us. He would have looked at all sort of Parliamentary issues which had a certain moral aspect to them – nuclear armaments – things of that nature. He was also a very strong supporter of capital punishment and could give the moral arguments for taking that line. He was genuine and sincere and he was never arrogant about other people who differed from him in the application of his principles to any particular issue."

Bradford's party leader recalls the morning of his murder: "We were in party headquarters for a special meeting of the party executive to go through the new constitution and rules. We were making good progress when Jean Coulter came in and up the table to me. She whispered in my ear that Robert had been shot so I said 'that's bad Jean but go and take your seat and we will check on it'. I asked Sir George Clarke if he would go because I felt that if I dashed out it would attract too much attention. He went and rang the police and got the sad confirmation that indeed he had been shot dead. So I passed a note to the late Michael Armstrong who was on his feet explaining the rules and asked that he stop at an appropriate moment. Then I intervened and said 'we want to give you the sad and shocking news that our colleague Robert Bradford has been murdered in Finaghy'. Of course there were cries of astonishment, shock, and grief. Then I said 'it would probably be in the mind of all of you that we should now adjourn this meeting'. Obviously everyone immediately agreed.

"I asked the officers to remain while I made an appointment to see the duty minister at Stormont who, that weekend, was Nicholas Scott. I simply said to the troops that the news was going to be as big a shock to the people in the constituencies as it had been to us and as they were the key people I would like them to go back to their homes and constituencies and calm people as best they could. I, along with Harold McCusker, Michael Armstrong and Ken Maginnis, went to see Scott. The meeting lasted about an hour and was very stormy."

The shock waves and sorrow did indeed sweep across the Province and a day of protest was organised for the following Monday. The country came to a standstill as services and rallies were held in memory of Bradford. Molyneaux stayed for a short time at the City Hall rally in Belfast which saw the dramatic arrival of barrister Robert McCartney on to the political scene when he grabbed the microphone from DUP leader Ian Paisley.

The Ulster Unionist leader was due to speak at a rally in Limavady, then Londonderry and Claudy. He remembers arriving in Derry with the Waterside district completely still and silent.

"I parked the car there, for in those days I was still driving myself, and started to walk towards Craigavon Bridge. It was absolutely deserted apart from a couple of policemen stopping what traffic there was. I was all by myself and I could see a crowd stretched out at the other end of the bridge. All of a sudden they started cheering and clapping and I couldn't work out what it was all about. Then I realised it was for me, well not for Jim Molyneaux personally, but they were delighted to see someone from the east of the Province had arrived. They then ran across the bridge, shaking my hands and someone even lifted me up and carried me to the other end where I had to make an impromptu speech. That over, I declined all offers of food and was escorted back to retrieve my car because of my need to reach a meeting in Claudy. I eventually got home well after midnight, a little weary, and that's what I can remember of that day."

In the aftermath of Bradford's murder Molyneaux, as leader, was exhorted to do a variety of things which he knew his dead colleague would simply not have approved of. He knew he had to take account of people's shock and grief but he had to, out of necessity, look ahead. This he attempted to do by having several top level meetings in London with Government Ministers and senior security officers in the hope that there would be some change in the Conservative Government's attitude towards terrorism in Northern Ireland.

However he faced criticism from within his own party and from outside that he should have stayed at home rather than what they felt was his fleeing to London. It is a criticism which has been levelled at him on many occasions since.

Behind all of this he also had to cope with his own grief: "I think it was made worse because I felt more isolated simply because I was conscious, even then, that people were not fully comprehending my obsession with the need to keep a grip of yourself no matter how deeply you are hurt".

This obsession of his was evident again in the aftermath of Edgar Graham's murder. The young law lecturer at Belfast's Queen's University was shot dead at point blank range as he chatted to a colleague near the university on the morning of December 7, 1983. He had been a rising star in the Ulster Unionist Party, particularly because of his legal arguments about the extradition of terrorists from the Republic.

Molyneaux believes he would have eventually become the leader of the party and that his murder was one of the most calculated and coldly carried out in Northern Ireland.

He admits that he was angry on the day of the young lawyer's funeral: "It had been a very dignified and moving service in Randalstown. After the committal, the ladies of the church had, very kindly, laid on tea and sandwiches. But after about ten minutes in the hall I said to Norman Hutton, 'I think action has got to be taken to quell some of these mourners'. It was because it was becoming like a parish social, in a thoughtless kind of way, as they did not realise what they were doing. The noise was deafening. Norman agreed and I said somebody would have to thank the minister and ladies for their hospitality and I thought it was time to do it. So I stood up on the platform and simply said that I was sure everyone would want me to convey their appreciation for the cup of tea which 'made more bearable the grief which had stricken every heart present here in this hall this afternoon'. There was a sort of hush, people started to look at each other and they started to melt away.

I know it was a bit like what happens, I suppose, after any funeral, people saying to each other 'oh, I haven't seen you since so and so's wedding'. But they did not realise that around 120 of such conversations was making the most fearful din. Then you looked up and sitting in the corner was Edgar's father, mother, sister and relatives just completely broken. I suppose that is my view and it makes me unpopular on such occasions."

He rejects any suggestion that he has had an inner strength to continue as normal during such ordeals. Instead he maintains it is a strength which had been fed into him.

"It is fed into you by the fact that you are conscious that everybody is looking to you for a lead, watching very closely how you are going to react and then that has a bearing on how they are going to behave. So that is why you have got to do the stiff upper lip operation – simply because of that. It is also not necessarily put on; it is because you recognise that you have a responsibility. It is the same in wartime that even if you are frightened out of your wits you must not show it because if you do it is infectious."

It is something he has tried to apply ever since his own experiences in war but sometimes the thin lip does quiver – either with sorrow or anger such as in this small incident immediately after Edgar Graham's murder. He returned hurriedly from London and arrived at Aldergrove to be confronted by a persistent television journalist. In his hurry to speak to the Ulster Unionist leader, a lead he was using tripped up his intended interviewee. This made the temper rise but it was not vented until the same journalist asked what Molyneaux regarded as a "damned silly question" a little later.

"It was something like 'would this murder tempt me into retiring from politics', I'm afraid I let fly at him and used a few choice words as well."

But in typical fashion he adds: "I think maybe that was something I should not have done – but it was only natural".

3. Home

The lot of a backbencher in one of the two main British political parties is soul destroying. This sounds a strange view coming from someone who has spent almost 20 years in the corridors of Westminster. But Jim Molyneaux hold no thoughts of grandeur about the place where he has worked since June 1970.

"You are never told why you are voting in a certain way and if you ask you are told to mind your own business – particularly if you are in the party of government. It is not because you know you are only a small cog – it is the fact of not knowing what is going on and why certain decisions have been taken."

When he arrived on the floor of the House of Commons, Molyneaux had immediately taken the Conservative whip as did all Unionists in those days when the names of the two parties were still linked.

Ted Heath was Prime Minister, Francis Pym his government's chief whip. Molyneaux remembers that the first burst of enthusiasm died quickly among some Conservative contemporaries who soon became disillusioned with the system. He joined the 1922 Committee which would usually have about 150 members in its ranks. They meet every Thursday evening from 6.00 pm to around 6.17 pm. Nothing has changed since he was in their midst.

"The duty whip comes along, not even the chief whip, and tells them how they should vote during the next week's proceedings. Never why – just the procedure which they should follow," he outlines.

This is why he finds the present equal citizenship campaign unrealistic. One of its fallacies, he claims, is the belief that if it succeeded in returning 10 members to the House of Commons in either of the major parties, Northern Ireland would receive a better hearing in the Mother of Parliaments.

"The exact opposite would happen, no matter how good or conscientious the MPs were. The farming lobby within the Conservative Party is by far and away the largest Parliamentary grouping. But even three weeks before the 1987 General Election, the then Agriculture Minister Michael Jopling, backed up by Mrs Thatcher, told this body of MPs that they were to tell their farming constituents to stop 'digging for victory', stop producing cereals and plant trees instead. They had to take it, about 120 of them – nearly half the Parliamentary party. So, far from improving and strengthening Northern Ireland's leverage in Parliament, it would weaken it by submerging members into either of the two big bodies where they have absolutely no say and where they are never consulted about anything."

During his time on the backbenches Molyneaux too felt the wrath of the system. He received a letter on November 29, 1972 from Francis Pym, pointing out that the Government had had a very poor majority on a two-line whip and wanted an explanation from the member for Antrim South as to why he had not been there.

A reply was sent to the chief whip's office in 10 Downing Street on December 4. In it the Ulster Unionist leader said he had given his support to the Government since he had entered Parliament until its "initiative" on the Province on March 24, that year. (This was the abolition of Stormont and its replacement by direct rule).

The letter continued: "But so great has been the sense of betrayal that such support must, at times take second place to my duty to do what I can in the constituency to ease the sufferings which result from the mistaken policies of the Government".

Pym, on another occasion, tried to woo his backbenchers by holding a small dinner party. Among the selected numbers were Jim Molyneaux and Winston Churchill. During the conversation over the table Molyneaux put his point of how shamefully backbenchers were treated.

The chief whip matter of factly replied that everyone went through such a phase but the situation changed as soon as a member was appointed to the government.

"But, I said, I am not ambitious about becoming a member of the Government. What I do believe is that we, here around this table, are entitled to know the reasons why we are being asked to vote for certain government policies which we have had no part in shaping. I think he regretted inviting me as the others then became quite indignant.

Quite frankly I was in a cast iron position to complain as I did not want to push myself for a government post. I never had the wildest expectations of becoming involved like that as the price you then pay for being in the Government is that you become muzzled. Even if you are on the lowest tier of the government you cannot criticise it. This would mean that you could not arrive at a constituency meeting in South Antrim and attack the Government over its security policy. You are neutered. I know I would never have been in such a position anyway and I never had any intention of becoming involved – even as a junior whip.

Only those with inquiring minds who have nothing to lose would ever dare to suggest that they should be consulted and that there should be a greater degree of democracy. Even then they would go down in the chief whip's little black book and when he and the Prime Minister are plotting out a Government reshuffle, the individual's name would crop up and the chief whip would say 'well no, he is competent but he tends to be argumentative'. No matter how good you would have been at the job, you are cancelled out."

This view of having no intention of ever becoming totally immersed in a certain aspect of life has been prevalent in Molyneaux's thinking over the years. However the reality has been slightly different – circumstances and an element of being in the right place at the wrong time have worked against him.

He had no intention, for example, of becoming involved in the Unionist party after his demobilisation. He enjoyed returning home and began immediately in July 1946 to "get stuck in" again with the poultry venture. He also took a partnership in his uncle Jack Morrison's small printing firm in Crumlin. He believes the fact that he was doing two jobs – looking after the poultry first thing in the morning, then working normal business hours before returning to the farm – meant he had little time to dwell on what he had witnessed during the war. One night during each week he worked until 2.00 am changing trays in the electric incubator and at one stage there were more than 100 breeding turkey hens in the expanding business.

Molyneaux was also relieved to be home. The spit and polish aspect of service had been gradually dominating proceedings in the RAF – something he did not like.

"You could put up with all of it when there was a war on but I would have found it difficult to settle down to the insecurity and, in many ways, the dreariness, of service life. The fact that you were suddenly posted away from your own unit to another did not attract me. You were simply allocated a bed space, a kit bag and a locker and over a weekend you could have found it all transferred 400 miles away. There was no such thing as a home away from home. When you had your fill of that in your early 20's it was a relief, in many ways, to become settled again at home."

The involvement with politics began, by accident, just three months after his return. Like his father and grandfather, he was a member of the Orange Order. After a lodge meeting on a Saturday night in

September, a friend, Joe Whiteside, asked him to return to the Ballynadrenta hall the following Wednesday night to help him sort out a faulty heating system.

Molyneaux dutifully went and on arriving found that a meeting of the remnants of the Diamond Women's Unionist branch which was put on ice during the war, was underway. As is a traditional aspect of life throughout Northern Ireland tea was brewing and the two young men were asked if they would like to sit in and await a cuppa. When they did the small band of women were discussing where they had left off before the war. Somebody suggested that rather than keep the branch exclusively female, it should be mixed. Of course the two men in the room had not been paying too much attention to what was going on, they were simply waiting for that cup of tea.

"They were talking about the election of officers and they immediately appointed a president, a fairly prominent member of the old branch. They then turned their attention to the chairman's position. I remember several of them said 'well, now that we are a mixed branch why don't we have a male chairman'. It was almost like well you will do and somebody proposed me. I looked around and pointed out to the small gathering that I had only returned and did not know the local situation very well. The attitude was then one of 'we will all learn together' and I was elected chairman there and then – all because I had sat waiting for a cup of tea."

He maintains he never realised what the ramifications were going to be – more than 40 years in Unionist politics.

"We were an isolated, country area. It was a small branch in a small community, so you never thought of the bigger world outside. It never dawned on me what was going to happen."

A few weeks later the process of becoming more and more immersed in the administrative side of Unionist politics began. He received an invitation to go to a meeting of the Antrim division association's management committee. This went well and he was then asked to go to the association's annual meeting. Within a year, because of an organisational change, he was assistant secretary, then divisional secretary for Antrim. In turn this entitled him to be a delegate at the then South Antrim Imperial Unionist Association meetings.

In 1948 under the Attlee Government the Representation of the People Act abolished the university representation at Westminster. This seat had been held by Sir Douglas Savoury who was a French Professor at Queen's. He decided to seek election in South Antrim and did so in 1949. Molyneaux became involved in this process as a sub-agent for the Antrim division. It was his first "operational" job with the Unionist Party and one which he found interesting. He was still, however, unconscious of the fact that he was becoming more and more involved as a cog in the political wheel. The poultry farming and the printing work continued while evenings were turned over to administrative work for the Unionist Party.

One new aspect to the election process was his organisation of transport to polling stations. He ruled out other people's suggestions that voters could find their own way: "There was always this temptation of people saying 'but sure so and so can come with their next door neighbour, he has a car'. In reply I always said that this was not the point, we wanted their vote and if we were to persuade them to make the effort to go the poll then we should provide transport if they needed it".

Savoury served as MP until 1955 when he retired. During this time Molyneaux remained as the Antrim divisional secretary and chairman of the Diamond branch. However he eventually gave up this position so that someone else could take on the duties. It is something he believes should be applied in all walks of life.

"It has always been my policy not to hold on to jobs. If you move up the ladder, or are pushed up it, then you should not cling onto the previous one because you are blocking off the line of promotion for other people coming on. There is a temptation for people to do that and I think it is wrong-headed, you have to make way for younger folk coming behind."

Three hopefuls came forward for selection as the new Unionist candidate – two barristers, John Megaw from Ballymoney, Cambridge boxing champion Knox Cunningham while the third was Richard Body who eventually became Sir Richard, chairman of the House of Commons select committee on agriculture. Cunningham got the nomination and again Molyneaux became sub-agent for the Antrim division in the 1955 election.

His first contact with the new candidate came in the run-up to the poll when he took him on a tour of his patch. The barrister was duly elected and during his firm term in Parliament, Molyneaux became treasurer of the Imperial Association in South Antrim.

Throughout this period Molyneaux never noticed any handicap in his being a farmer's son. The social gap had diminished thanks to the war and he was never conscious of the fact that the Unionist artistocracy, in the past, had held all the key positions within the party – whether at Stormont or Westminster.

Cunningham's family, for example, came from Parkgate outside

Antrim and had arrived from Ayrshire during the Williamite wars. He was educated at the Royal Belfast Academical Institution, Fetter College and Clare College, Cambridge where he was heavyweight boxing champion in 1931. He was called to the Bar, Middle Temple, in 1939, and to the Inn of the Court, Northern Ireland in 1942.

In contrast Jim Molyneaux was the son of a not well-to-do farmer, had had a public elementary education and war service. While his grandfather had always expressed great interest in national politics no one in the family had ever been actively involved.

"I never felt any inverted snobbery. I never had any chip on my shoulder. I simply said I am going to be myself and they can either accept or reject it. After I became leader it was pointed out in a newspaper that the Unionist Party had come down in the world as the new man did not come from the big house. It was blunt but it was the truth."

Cunningham was appointed Parliamentary Private Secretary to Harold Macmillan in 1959. Many in the constituency looked upon this as a great honour – their MP now had the ear of the Prime Minister and was, in many ways, his right hand man.

However John Harbinson, in his book The Ulster Unionist Party, 1882–1973, points out that since 1921 no Unionist has held any significant office in a Conservative Government. He cites the fact that while Cunningham, along with Ronald Ross and the late Duke of Westminster, had been PPS's this was the "sum total of their achievement". They have indeed been political nonentities who have left no real mark on either the House of Commons at Westminster or the Conservative Party."

There was also a growing annoyance in South Antrim that as PPS Cunningham was not paying enough attention to constituency matters. In his position he was unable to speak in the House of Commons as it would have been presumed that he was reflecting the views of the Prime Minister.

This agitation grew until there was a split in the constituency party and he was challenged for selection in 1963. His opponent was Roy Bradford. Molyneaux, as constituency treasurer, along with the president remained loyal to the sitting MP but the others including the chairman Doagh man Alex McConnell backed the future Stormont Minister. The vote was two to one in favour of Cunningham.

Molyneaux remembers the final moments of the meeting which was held in the old party building in Glengall Street in Belfast.

"Alex said 'well, that's it decided, we must put the past behind us and look to the future. Knox got up, in that quiet way of his, and thanked the chairman for his congratulations. But he continued 'you, Mr Chairman have quite rightly said that we must put the past behind us and look to the future. That means that you will have to go as I must have a chairman who is going to be loyal to me as a member' and he then went over the same advice to the other defecting officers. In one way or another they did go. It was a typical Knox way of doing things – ever so quietly but in a determined style. A normal sort of politician would not have done it that way, he would have dithered over it and decided that everyone should come together. However Knox's clear cut reasoning was that if people defected once, then they could defect again and he wanted to know where he stood. It was not that he wanted to be surrounded by yes men but at least he wanted people around who were not working against him. It was as clear cut as that."

In the wake of this Molyneaux became honorary secretary of the South Antrim Imperial Association.

The Profumo affair eventually brought down the Macmillan Government to be replaced by the short-lived Douglas-Home administration. Molyneaux believes he wanted to keep Cunningham on as his PPS but the South Antrim MP felt that he would always be comparing him with his former master, so he declined.

1964 saw a General Election and Harold Wilson was installed as occupier of No 10. Cunningham returned to the backbenches where he spent the remaining six years of his Parliamentary career. Molyneaux maintains that this played a key part in his shock decision not to run in the 1970 election.

"There he had been knowing everything that was going on, beside the Prime Minister daily and then he was not in the circle anymore. It was bound to have a bearing on his final decision." Another factor was that he was suspicious of Ted Heath and told Molyneaux, as the tensions began to build up in Northern Ireland in 1969, "You are going to find that man Heath no friend of Ulster".

During his 15 years in Parliament he had become quite a controversial character, certainly right-wing, and had had many clashes with Harold Wilson during the Labour administration. He also had, very vocally, opposed the O'Neill – Lemass, O'Neill – Lynch meetings, a stand emphatically backed by his constituency secretary.

The "administrator" himself ruffled a few feathers shortly after the historical step which saw the Prime Minister of Northern Ireland inviting his Dublin counterpart Sean Lemass to lunch at Stormont on January 14, 1965.

Harbinson again on The Ulster Unionist Party, said Terence O'Neill's action was received favourably by the general public, but he was severely criticised by elements within his own ranks. One of them was Jim Molyneaux. The following month O'Neill paid a visit to Dublin and as a result a series of inter-departmental and inter-Ministerial discussions got underway on matters of mutual interest.

The South Antrim constituency secretary delivered a speech in Lisburn about the state of affairs. He pointed out that while it was proper and legitimate for Prime Ministers to meet to discuss such matters of mutual interest, there could be constitutional dangers in permitting civil servants to meet and discuss matters of government. Nothing, he notes, has changed in more than 20 years.

After the speech a row erupted over his remarks. The advice arrived to him from party headquarters that he should clarify the speech and retract certain parts of it. He refused to do so, stating that if he had not meant it he would not have said it.

While he was only a constituency secretary and, as he describes himself "small beer" at that time, he grasped any opportunity he had to speak to the Prime Minister and warn him of what he saw as the serious risks O'Neill was taking.

The Prime Minister had told the Ulster Unionist Council "Our task will be literally to transform Ulster. To achieve it will demand bold and imaginative measures". Molyneaux agreed with this as he felt Northern Ireland had to adjust to the changing world around it. But he was concerned about the way Terence O'Neill handled the situation, even if the latter realised that after the Lemass meeting he was going to be in trouble.

In his autobiography he noted: "I helped Mr Lemass off with his coat and suggested that after his long drive he would probably like to wash his hands. Eventually in the rather spacious loo at Stormont House he suddenly said, 'I shall get into terrible trouble for this'. 'No, Mr Lemass,' I replied, 'it is I who will get into trouble for this".

Molyneaux's considered view of the historic episode was that the Ulster Prime Minister went about it in the wrong way.

"If you are going to engage in that kind of thing you must ensure that it does not lead to mistrust. What you do is that you make certain that people trust you absolutely. They know why you are advocating certain courses, that you explain it carefully to them and that you take them into your confidence. You can do that with a political party because if you go to the party executive, for example, put your cards on the table face up and say to them 'this is how I think we should deal with it' then they will talk about it and in the end you will get a consensus view. This will take you a little way along the road to progress and modernising policies.

However I believe what a leader must not do is to be influenced by people who do not have their feet on the ground. There are those who do not understand how politics work or its mechanisms but, with their influence, you find a leader launching out with some startling departure from a previously agreed policy. This simply leaves the troops bewildered and a long way behind him. In turn this creates the most dangerous situation in any political structure and that involves uncertainty and instability.

An example of it with Terence O'Neill was the actual invitation to Lemass. It was kept secret so not only was the Cabinet not consulted but individual members were not told about it until they were invited to Stormont. Only then did some of them, for the first time, realise that the Prime Minister of the Irish Republic was in their midst. You cannot do things like that."

Molyneaux suggests that because of O'Neill's own aloofness he was unable to gauge what the man in the street was really thinking about such moves which would have balanced the more theoretical policies being put forward by advisers. This view, in some respects, is confirmed by Harbinson. He noted: "He appears to have been unwilling, or unable, to mix freely with his fellow Unionists, either inside or outside Parliament. He took his advice from the professional administrators rather than the junta at party headquarters . . . and his aloofness acquired for him, rightly or wrongly, a reputation of being a difficult colleague".

The Ulster Unionist leader continued in his administrative role throughout the mounting crisis which eventually erupted on the streets of Londonderry on October 5, 1968. The farming and printing business continued as did his duties as an Antrim County councillor, a post he had been elected to in 1964. One of the major constituency jobs he had to carry out from time to time was the delivery of speeches on behalf of the absent MP.

Air travel in those days was still, in some ways, haphazard. If there was fog at Heathrow Molyneaux would receive a call from Cunningham to say he could not make the flight and would he mind going to a certain meeting on his behalf. The secretary never realised that this proved to be part of his political training.

However nothing could have prepared him for the bombshell which was presented to him on Monday May 17, 1970. Harold Wilson had indicated that he was going to call a General Election. In his traditional manner the secretary who became election agent for the hustings period, had already the "machine" well oiled and ready to go. All that was needed was the date.

On the Sunday night the sitting MP rang his agent unexpectedly with the request that he meet him at the airport on the following afternoon. Molyneaux was bewildered by this as it was still too early for the candidate to begin canvassing. He also knew that in the final days of a Parliament before a General Election there was a frantic rush to get Government legislation passed and Cunningham would be busy at Westminster.

In spite of questioning the wisdom of such a move, he eventually agreed to the request and met the MP at Aldergrove.

"He looked pretty thoughtful when I met him. Then the bombshell came. Just as I drove out onto the old airport road, Knox said to me in that quiet voice 'I want you to be the first to know, I am not going'. I suppose my immediate reaction, as agent, was instinctively something like we have less than a month to go before a general election, how on earth are we going to get a candidate within that time. It was an immediate reaction as an agent, not as a politician. Of course I immediately asked him what I was going to do now without a candidate and the reply came back that that was up to me and the chairman, not him."

Molyneaux maintains that the thought of himself did not even briefly cross his mind. He saw himself as the mechanism through which the election process was organised and he took a certain pride in his work in what was the largest constituency in the United Kingdom.

"That was my main aim – to run a smooth operation and to achieve a good result at the end of it. It was as simple as that."

Cunningham requested that he drove to Carrickfergus to see the constituency chairman Sam Steele. He did so in a daze and met an even more puzzled Mr Steele in his living room.

"Knox again quietly said 'I have told Jim on the way over and now I want you, as my chairman, to know that I am not standing'. Sam said 'You are not what! What do you mean you are not standing and what are we going to do without a candidate now that the date has been set'. (Wilson had just announced it was to be June 18). Knox pointed out that constitutionally he could not interfere in the process and as the two senior officers it was up to us to get it organised. He then handed Sam an official note to read to the management committee and left to go back to the car noting that he could not properly be involved in any further discussions. Sam must have stood and stared at the closed door for three or four minutes before I said to him that we had work to do. We got out the rule book to see how we could summon an emergency management committee meeting within three days."

One was organised for May 22 at Ballyhill Orange Hall, near Nutts Corner, while the agent without a candidate continued with the preparation for an election. The management committee received the news with the predictable surprise. The chairman informed them that he had felt it prudent, earlier that day, to inform Sir George Clarke, the then chairman of the party's standing committee, of the shock move. He pointed out that a quick decision had to be made as to who would be the Unionist candidate and that Sir George had suggested the election agent – one Jim Molyneaux.

"The members had caught on to this while I had kept my head down taking notes. I suddenly discovered that they had got this band going. I kept arguing with them that that was not their decision to make. I kept telling them that their function was to decide the arrangements and the date of a selection meeting. I gradually won them around to the view that everything had to be done in a proper and seemly manner. However they still went on that I should be the candidate and, in spite of protests, back came the reply that they would recommend me to the selection meeting. By this stage I decided that they were all getting too excited and I should leave so they could come to a calm, reasonable decision."

He left and went and sat in his car. Only then did it strike him as to what was happening. It was the arguments put forward by the committee which were now dawning on him. As a body, members said he knew the constituency better than anyone because of his work as secretary and election agent; he had deputised for Cunningham on many occasions and so because of the situation he was the obvious choice.

"Before I left I told them that I had not been given the opportunity to decide whether I wanted to do it or not. But they rejected this out of hand, pointing out that the party had to win the seat, this was my own objective and therefore I had a duty to do it. I was told I had to put my own wishes away.

"As I sat in the car I could not concentrate. But the kind of argument they were putting forward made me realise that there was likely to be no escape."

After 15 minutes Mrs Gertie Linton, the association's vice-chairman, came out, tapped the window and told him that members had sentenced him in his absence.

"I went back in again, at which point they horrified me, for they all jumped up in a standing ovation. I was then informed that they were to recommend my selection. Again I told them it was not their job, others had every right to come forward. I also pointed out that I could no longer be honorary secretary and resigned on the spot. I thought that might have brought them to their senses but it did not. It would have been grossly improper if they were determined to put me forward at the selection meeting, for me to continue in that position. I put the pen down and sat with my arms folded for the rest of the meeting."

The Cunningham decision was recorded in the Belfast News Letter the following morning under the headline "Polls shock: Sir Knox to Quit". It pointed out that it had astonished several of his Westminster colleagues. But while Molyneaux too was dumbfounded by the news, he began to analyse what really had been the central reason for the decision to retire. The explanation given to the press was that for health reasons he wanted to go. He had been badly injured during the Second World War when he served in the Scots Guards.

However Molyneaux believes that after serving as PPS to Macmillan he never really enjoyed being confined to the backbenches with no real role to play. He also, as suggested before, felt he could not work under Ted Heath.

"I detected something a couple of years before he decided to go that while he was still devoted to his constituents, he was driving himself to do his job rather than doing it with any real enthusiasm."

The selection meeting was held on a warm June 1 evening in the same hall as the fateful management gathering. Only one other man put his name forward, a young lawyer practising in London with family connections in County Tyrone. More than 300 attended and the two novices awaited their call to address the meeing. It was being chaired by the then party secretary Jim Bailie.

It was all being held against a background of growing criticism of the Prime Minister Major James Chichester-Clark. Joint working parties of Stormont and Westminster civil servants, had been established under the Callaghan Reforms and it was becoming clearer that more and more political decisions were being taken out of the hands of the Stormont Government by referring them to these bodies. Under Chichester-Clark, Unionists witnessed the reform of the RUC as suggested in the Hunt Report, the "B" Specials were disbanded and the Prevention of Incitement to Hatred Act was introduced. Some within the party did not want to accept any of it and several commentators noted the traumatic experience the Unionist Party was going through.

The right wing led by Bill Craig and Harry West along with Ian Paisley's Protestant Unionist Party used the division to criticise the decision to disband the "B" Specials and disarm the RUC – particularly as violence was escalating.

A lone voice sitting in a gallery box in the Orange hall, demanded to know from the would-be candidate Molyneaux if he would unreservedly support the Prime Minister.

"I jumped to my feet and said 'Indeed I will not' at which point there was a gasp of astonishment around the place. I then said I was sure the gathering would not expect me to go to Westminster and support Harold Wilson. My job was to get him out. This received thunderous applause. The man, of course, pointed out that he was not referring to Wilson but to Chichester-Clark and laughter echoed around the room. Jim Bailie said that time was up and that was it. Afterwards a relative of mine noted that Jim had not answered the question but an association member pointed out that the way he did had convinced him that they were on to a winner." He won the selection by an overwhelming majority.

The pattern was repeated on June 18. In a 67 per cent poll of 144,743 electors, Molyneaux had a majority of 39,618. His closest rival was Northern Ireland Labour candidate Robert Johnston with 19,971.

He did not realise that throughout the campaign both family and close friends were worried about the attacks being levelled at him from other candidates. The Independent Unionist candidate Tom Caldwell who was already a Stormont MP for Willowfield, Belfast, continually challenged him on issues and accused him of being an under-cover Paisleyite. In his election communication he pointed out that the "Official Unionist candidate is backed by Paisley. He obviously intends to woo the moderate vote as well. He will show two faces. This is politically dishonest." It continued: "None of the other candidates can possibly expect to defeat the Paisley candidate. In other words, in this particular election, whatever your political views, you must vote for me".

Molyneaux explains that it was only afterwards that he realised how tense and worried family and friends were: "These challenges came day after day and I simply did not respond. No one seemed to understand that each time it was the name Molyneaux which was placed in front of them, not the challenger's; therefore I did not have to do anything. It was Molyneaux who was being projected. What worried the family was that they felt I was not defending my own corner. They believed I was being too complacent and could not understand why I was allowing all of this criticism to flow over me. The challenges kept coming, for example, about my political allegiance and I was asked to comment by the press. My simple reply was 'Who is Mr Caldwell?' It stuck until polling day".

After the seven hour count there was little celebration on the part of the new MP. He went to an already arranged meeting and left the rejoicing behind. There was also little elation when he arrived at Westminster. He had been there on several occasions before and had already realised through work with Cunningham that he might only be able to win one out of three constituency cases against bureaucracy.

"I was also 49 so I did not go there as a starry eyed idealist. To be truthful it was not that much of a thrill. Even the building did not impress me." It also helped that he was a bachelor: "You had the freedom to decide that if your duties required you, you could put aside all considerations of a private life. It has meant that with the resulting, increasing pressure through becoming Parliamentary leader and then party leader that you can say 'right you have a job to do, get on with it'. The fact that you have no one to consider or to consult means your decision making can be crisper than it would otherwise be."

However there has also been the disadvantage that he has missed family life. The Molyneaux family through nieces and nephews have contributed a great deal. But a gap is there – particularly at holiday time.

"Other people are doing things but I have got into this kind of rut that when I do have time off I devote it to some aspect of the job. There is always a backlog of adminstrative stuff to do. Then I miss having a family of my own."

Once in Parliament he took his time before delivering his Maiden Speech, he arrived in late June with just a month before the summer recess; many new members were rushing to make their impact so he felt it inadvisable to join the queue. His name came up to be the first speaker in the debate on the Consolidated Fund Bill (Northern Ireland) on February 15, 1971. As a topic he felt it right, with the increasing emergence of the Provisional IRA, to highlight the duties of the Home Secretary, Reginald Maudling, to the people of Northern Ireland.

He flew over on the eve of the debate, a Sunday, and before continuing his scribblings in the living room, went to the bedroom and turned on the electric blanket. Shortly afterwards going to the kitchen, he passed the bedroom and smelt smoke. The blanket had gone on fire and a blue circle of smoke was spiralling towards the ceiling. That put an end to the speech writing.

He was nervous in the way he still would be before delivering a major speech either to his party conference or the annual meeting of the Ulster Unionist Council. The speech highlighted that, for the first time, the public was witnessing in Western Europe a demonstration of urban guerilla warfare. He also rejected a possible solution to the Northern Ireland troubles which had found general favour.

"The first and most popular solution is the suggestion of getting the three Governments round a table. That is an attractive but futile idea since the IRA and their anarchist friends are utterly opposed to all three Governments. They are equally hostile to Stormont and to Dublin. What possible good could come of any agreement reached between the three Governments", he said.

After the speech he took up advice given to him by his predecesor who told him that an MP should not talk too frequently, or sign too many early day motions or put down too many written questions as he devalued himself and the importance of the opportunities. He holds this view to today and has found that people will pay more attention when someone who holds to this rule does speak rather than attempting to seek continual publicity. He found too the routine and procedures relatively simple to follow and was never overawed by the institution.

Molyneaux had gone to an Orange hall to look at a heating system. Now more than 20 years later he was sitting on a green bench in the Mother of Parliaments. Yet he had never refused to get away from the process through which he had travelled to reach his unplotted destination. There has to be a question as to why he never did say no.

"You do ask why it happencd and I cannot exactly answer. All those years of constituency work. During all those years of constituency work it was not unusual at the end of a day's work to go out to a meeting, arrive home after midnight and settle down to addressing envelopes when sensible people would have gone to bed. Yet I took it all in my stride and I have never worked out why I ended up where I did. There is an unexplained factor about it all. I think it is to do with the old adage of 'being in the right place at the right time'. My problem has always been that I have been in the right place at the wrong time.

"Nearly everything which has happened to me in my political career has happened by sheer accident. I did not voluntarily take on jobs, I happened to be in a position where I could not legitimately argue that I could not do it. For example, if Harry West had not lost the Fermanagh seat in October 1974, then I would have gone on being whip at Westminster – not leader. Then it was repeated when Harry resigned as party leader – in spite of my entreaties.

"It is not a question of saying 'there is a job, if I am proposed for that I will take it'. It is indeed the opposite. A job appeared and I found I did not have any choice and was told so frequently. It is something I have never been able to analyse. I am not daft enough to believe it is ability apart from a recognition that I have a mind of my own; that I do not treat people in an abrasive way and that, maybe, I am a common denominator."

The situation has been repeated on several occasions and fate maybe has played its part in steering him from a small, country Unionist branch to becoming leader of the Ulster Unionist Party and a Privy Counsellor. Otherwise he cannot explain it.

4. Back Bencher

Former Prime Minister Ted Heath told the House of Commons on December 16, 1976 that a speech made by Jim Molyneaux in the same surroundings three days earlier had been a "major statement and that it was very important in terms of future progress" for Northern Ireland.

They had always been adversaries so this remark, made during the Second Reading of the Scotland and Wales Bill, was praise indeed. He went further by noting that Molyneaux's speech "could lead to political progress in Northern Ireland".

Others, however, were not as sure about the positive element in the speech including Molyneaux's party leader Harry West. The South Antrim MP, as his contribution to the devolution debate, had emphasised that the devolution which mattered and had always mattered in Northern Ireland was not legislative but administrative.

"It is the lack of control over the application and execution of the law which is intolerable to us and which places our citizens at a crying disadvantage compared with all the rest of the United Kingdom", he told the House.

"Once this is understood, the old difficulties about power-sharing and widespread acceptance present themselves in a different and more amenable light, for it is essentially legislative and not administrative devolution which raised the dilemma between the irreconcilable ultimate objectives in Ulster and rendered insistence upon majority rule as an essential to one side as it was unacceptable to the other. This made devolution either a Loyalist talisman or a Republican backdoor, instead of being what it should have been – an essential guarantee of good government for the whole population."

The speech continued: "Ulster needs a regional government now. It needs a regional government in which – as in the present government of metropolitan regions in England – all political parties would automatically participate in proportion to their elected representation . . . In Ulster, the way is now clear for a start in devolving administration".

His views were officially recorded but no one made any comment until Ted Heath rose to speak – then all hell broke loose.

Molyneaux had been working in tandem with party leader Harry West since he became Unionist chief at Westminster in 1974. West had lost the Fermanagh and South Tyrone seat in the October General Election of that year and the reins were taken up by Molyneaux. They worked well enough together with regular and frequent telephone calls across the Irish Sea on top of the statutory party meetings. But their characters, as well as their appearances, were completely different.

West was from the established well-to-do Unionist background. An extensive farmer he had been, along with Brian Faulkner, the youngest member of the Brookeborough Cabinet of the late Fifties and early Sixties and regarded Stormont as the pinnacle of politics. He was blunt and forthright with a distinctive will of his own.

Molyneaux, on the other hand, was slight and shy. A backroom boy made good who had infinite patience and came across as being old before his time. He had never served at Stormont and never regarded it, as others did, as being on a similar power footing as Westminster.

West's main aim was the return of a devolved administration to Northern Ireland. It was also Molyneaux's, but that speech in December 1976 put him on an integration hook which he has been unable to wriggle off ever since.

The major problem between the two men was that while both had the same objective they, because of their personal make-up, went about trying to achieve it in totally different ways.

Party policy was for devolution as it had been outlined in the Convention Report of 1975. This majority backed paper had called for the restoration to a new devolved government the powers conferred on Stormont by the 1920 Act. Minority participation in government would be only in departmental committees and not the Cabinet. Westminster refused to accept the report maintaining the majority paper did not meet the criteria set out in the White Paper which had set it up. The then Labour Secretary of State Merlyn Rees recalled it for a further month in January 1976 and asked it to think again but it eventually ended two months later without finding any further agreement acceptable to Westminster. West amplified this report by simply calling for a devolved Parliament at Stormont.

But Molyneaux's approach was different and the tactics he applied in 1976 have been used by him many times since – the most recent example being over the Anglo-Irish Agreement. He believed it was pointless demanding, in a forthright way, the return of Stormont. He knew that Government had no intention of returning Northern Ireland to some watered down version of the old system.

West was unable to wait quietly in the wings unlike Molyneaux who has the habit of waiting patiently for something to happen after he has made sure that it will and has manoeuvered accordingly. A straight-forward question to the Government of "Are you going to restore a government at Stormont" would have received an equally blunt "No".

However as Molyneaux noted: "If you go about it in another manner with phrases such as 'Look, this has gone on too long, you have got to start restoring responsibility to the elected representatives of Northern Ireland' then this, I believed, would not receive a blunt no. You could then begin to get that operation underway, you would then formulate a structure, then build on it and eventually have in place something as concrete as the former administration, but not of the same bearing.

"It was with that objective of starting the process and, hopefully, achieving that goal which made me make that speech and which, in turn, caused so much turmoil."

The interpretation in Northern Ireland was that the leader of the Ulster Unionists at Westminster would settle for a glorified county council and had abandoned full-blown devolution. West was faced with a series of questions demanding to know exactly what was party policy. Although there was no confrontation between the two men and no ill-feeling at the time, the former leader has not forgiven Molyneaux.

"I had the difficult task of leading the Unionist Party during the period in which the Labour Party was in office at Westminster. Our party's policy during this time was strictly as outlined in the Convention Report – the return of a devolved government with adequate safeguards for the minority. During the latter years of my leadership I discovered through sources at Westminster that at least some Ulster Unionist members, while supporting our party's policy at home, were making it known in London that we did not want devolution but total integration. The idea of integration had absolutely no support from any political party at Westminster but this campaign was undoubtedly weakening our case. I felt the carpet was being taken from under my feet. This activity was causing confusion in Unionist circles and that confusion still remains."

However West had also been known for a change of direction in his policy and attitude to his party leader. Six years before Molyneaux made his "administrative devolution" speech West had been at the forefront of the West Ulster Unionist Council. This large pressure group within the party defended what it viewed as traditional Union-ism. As well as demanding tougher security policies, it opposed the reduction in the powers of local councils under the Macrory report and the creation of the Northern Ireland Housing Executive. In spite of his high profile in that Council, West resigned from it in 1971 after he was offered the post of Minister of Agriculture in the new Brian Faulkner government – even though he had previously described the local authority reforms as "Faulkner's Fiddle".

He still maintains Molyneaux's speech did untold damage to the party: "I thought he was loyal until I found he was undermining me at Westminster by continually saying that we did not want devolution. By the end of my time as leader I was sick, sore and tired of this confusion and, in many ways, was glad to leave it behind me".

The former Glengall Street chief also believes Molyneaux is full of false modesty and always secretly desired his position. He remembers that Molyneaux stood against him for leadership in 1974 after Faulkner resigned.

Prior to the 1976 speech the backroom boy had continued his work at Westminster in his usual quiet, orderly manner. He continually adhered to Cunningham's advice of not speaking too often in the House and made sure he did not put down too many written questions.

He was still the junior member under the leadership of the London-derry MP Robin Chichester-Clark when the warning signals began to flow over the fall of Stormont. Molyneaux, along with the South Down MP Willie Orr, had attempted to warn the Northern Ireland Prime Minister of the mutterings in the corridors at Westminster. However he recalls the annual meeting of the Ulster Unionist Council just weeks before the fateful day in March 1972.

Faulkner read out a telegram from Ted Heath noting that there had been widespread press speculation that the Stormont Parliament was to be suspended. Heath's telegram ended by declaring that the press had been informed that this was pure speculation. The members applauded, viewing this statement as reassurance and a message of support from the British Prime Minister.

However the two MPs believed it confirmed their worst fears, knowing how Westminster felt after the shooting dead of 13 civilians in Londonderry that January. It was this single act which spurred the Government on to take security powers away from Stormont. Molyneaux remembers his feelings: "The two of us looked at one another and I asked Willie 'do you feel a chill going up your spine' and Willie replied by saying that I had described his condition perfectly. He added that it probably meant the end of Stormont. You see, Heath could have said these reports had absolutely no foundation. Instead he described them as speculation and in British politics speculation has a habit of becoming fact. We tried to tell Brian not to give in, that everyone was behind him and that we would do our bit at Westminster, but you had the uneasy feeling that the situation had already gone over the dam".

The inevitable did happen on March 23, 1972 after Faulkner had been summoned to London for talks with Heath for the second time within 36 hours and where he was informed that Stormont was to be prorogued for one year, the powers of the Northern Ireland Government to be carried out by a Secretary of State and that an administrative commission would help the Ulster Secretary in his work.

He felt he had no alternative but to resign and take his Cabinet with him. Molyneaux believed and still does that Faulkner acted too hastily and should have delayed his decision, informing Heath that he would have to return to Belfast to consult his Cabinet before reaching a conclusion on what he should do.

Molyneaux maintains that Faulkner should have come home, gone straight to Hillsborough and asked the Governor Lord Grey to dissolve the Stormont Parliament in readiness for a General Election to gauge if the people of Northern Ireland wanted direct rule or would have preferred the retention of Stormont with a reform package.

This, he claims, would have wrong footed the Government and Heath would have found it almost impossible to abolish Stormont as it would have been viewed as denying the Northern Ireland people free elections. He learnt afterwards from the then Home Secretary Reginald Maudling, who had attended the crucial London meetings, that this tactic was the one the Government had feared most and was relieved when Faulkner did not act upon it.

Maudling, however, pointed out to Molyneaux that the Prime Minister himself had not grasped the ramifications of such a move if Faulkner had made it.

"You see, if Brian, instead of acting immediately, had said to Heath that he needed to consult his Cabinet and stone walled him that way, he could have come home, gone to Hillsborough and I am sure the Governor would have had to grant his request."

"Faulkner could have fought the election on the basis of democracy, namely the will of the people, asking them to decide, Roman Catholic and Protestant, if they wanted to be ruled directly by Westminster or a reformed Government at Stormont.

I believe this would have put Heath in an almost impossible situation, as for him to then abolish Stormont would have meant him suppressing free elections in a democracy. He would have had no choice but to have allowed the election to go on. If he had done that then I know there would have been a decisive thumbs down to direct rule and a backing for a package of reforms for everyone in Northern Ireland."

Molyneaux claims Faulkner was alerted to such a move but had never considered it. He views the whole episode as a "failure of nerves on somebody's part" but does not apportion all the blame to the Northern Ireland Prime Minister.

"There was still an attitude of well, if Westminster speaks we have to go along with it or we would be in danger of threatening the Union. Of course we, at Westminster, knew that this would not have been the case because the House of Commons simply would have rejected any move to suppress free elections. The message, I am afraid, never got through to Stormont."

Heath made the historic statement to the House on the morning of Friday March 24. He told members: "Parliament will, therefore, be invited to pass before Easter a measure transferring all legislative and executive powers now rested in the Northern Ireland Parliament and Government to the United Kingdom Parliament and a United Kingdom Minister. This provision will expire after one year unless this Parliament resolves otherwise. The Parliament of Northern Ireland would stand prorogued but would not be dissolved".

He ended the statement by noting: "I would like to pay tribute to the determination with which the Prime Minister of Northern Ireland and his Government have sought to overcome the difficulties which have beset the Province; and the House will wish to acknowledge the spirit in which he has agreed to remain in office until our legislation has been enacted. We greatly regret that we were unable in the end to reach agreement with him. In the last resort, however, responsibility rests with the United Kingdom Government and Parliament; and her Majesty's Government would be abdicating that responsibility if in this critical situation we did not take the action which we believed to be right".

Molyneaux made little contribution to the ensuing debate on the Northern Ireland (Temporary Powers) Bill still being a junior member of the Unionist team. His only sarcastic note was to point out that Government Ministers', three weeks previously, had been indicating that it would not be a bad thing if Brian Faulkner were to go.

However the main speaker on the Friday morning was Chichester-Clark who noted that it would have been perhaps a "better and franker" approach on the part of the Government by having complete integration for Northern Ireland into the United Kingdom.

"Does my right hon. friend," he said, "realise that the decision emphasises something which many of us have recognised for a long time, the very great constitutional difficulties of being a Member of Parliament for Northern Ireland in this House, because of the inter-action between the two Governments? Does he realise that, whatever some of us may think, there will be some who will feel bound to consider very carefully and very seriously whether they have any mandate to support such a decision, or, indeed, a mandate to remain in this Parliament?"

Molyneaux describes the reaction at home as one of shock and absolute bewilderment. It even put him into a bad temper and on the morning of the Heath statement went so far as to tear up his Order paper to the amusement of Ian Paisley.

The Unionists were summoned to the Prime Minister's room after the proceedings in the House. Heath informed them that the proro-gation had been the most constructive thing to do, considering the circumstances. North Down member Jim Kilfedder asked him what the object of it all was and he received the cold reply "To end the violence of course".

The Molyneaux temper had not calmed. He informed Heath: "Prime Minister, as your judgement on this matter is so seriously flawed I see no point in remaining here". He got up, walked around the table, heard a sneering remark coming from behind so deliberately pulled the oak door harder as he left. The noise reverberated around the room.

Later Willie Orr informed him that he had two regrets, one was that he had not joined Molyneaux, the second was that the South Antrim MP had not been able to see the expression on Ted Heath's face as the door slammed.

But Chichester-Clark frowned upon the outburst and told Molyneaux it was not the "done thing" at Westminster to behave in such a manner. The junior MP replied that he realised this but that there was always a first time and that had been it.

The ten man grouping met and, under the chairmanship of Chichester-Clark, agreed that they would withdraw their support from the Conservative Government, no longer automatically obeying its whip. The move was approved unanimously, they would not indicate how they would vote from now on and the tactic was announced to the press.

However while Unionist opposition to the Government's decision was united in Northern Ireland, the Parliamentary team's fell apart over that final weekend in March.

When they returned the following week to debate the new legislation which was to usher in direct rule, the members found out that Chichester-Clark had accepted a ministerial post at Employment in the Government.

Molyneaux recalls the affect the move had on the grouping: "We found that the chairman, after putting forward the new tactics the previous Friday, had gone over to the other side. It did not knock the stuffing out of us but it did shatter the unity which we thought we had and it certainly eroded the cohesion within the Parliamentary grouping. You were then never really sure who else might go over. We had had absolutely no indication that this was what Robin was going to do so it did make you slightly suspicious as to who was going to be next".

But the entire traditional Ulster Unionist Party was falling apart. Molyneaux puts it mildly by describing it as being in a "state of flux" but also admits that, at one stage, he feared its total disintegration.

The cracks began to appear immediately after the fall of Stormont and the eventual publication by the Tory Government of the Northern Ireland Constitution Bill in the March of the following year. It proposed an Assembly, elected by proportional representation, and with Westminster retaining law and order. This eventually led to the power-sharing executive.

But in the interim a new force began to expand within Unionism – Bill Craig's Ulster Vanguard. He had called for a two day stoppage on March 27 and 28, as Westminster voted on the abolition of Stormont. Work throughout the Province came to a virtual standstill. Molyneaux, along with the other MPs, was at Westminster.

During the following weeks the spotlight continued to focus on Craig. Faulkner appeared to be losing his grip on the party. However many of Craig's supporters remained within the Unionist Party maintaining that there were no contradictions in being a member of both organisations. They felt they were justified in this view after Faulkner invited Craig to sit on a policy committee to consider talks with the Government over the restoration of Stormont. But the former Prime Minister was committed to the maintenance of the Union while Craig had bluntly spoken of the possibility of its severance.

Further ructions appeared in the autumn of that year after Willie Whitelaw had invited parties to a conference on the political future of Northern Ireland.

The policy document produced by the Unionist Party and known as Towards the Future, suggested a unicameral Northern Ireland Parliament of 100 members who would be elected on a simple majority vote.

There would be five Parliamentary committees with at least three being chaired by Opposition members. This Parliament would have control of security and there would be a Bill of Rights.

But some members, like Roy Bradford, the former Minister of Commerce, said he was unable to support the party's proposals. He claimed there were only two courses open to Unionists – they either accepted the authority of Westminster or oppose it. He was joined by Basil McIvor, the former Minister for Community Relations.

The situation became even more chaotic when the Green Paper, proposing the new Assembly, was published on October 30, 1972. Craig and his supporters rejected the right of the Government to change the Northern Ireland Constitution and emphasised that they would call for UDI if necessary.

Faulkner accepted the authority of Westminster but believed Ulster would only be safe it there was a return of a Stormont which had control over security matters. While the Bradford grouping continued to believe that Stormont would never return and who had decided the only way forward was through power-sharing.

As for Molyneaux, he like others had backed Craig's strong, vocal opposition to the abolition of Stormont. But when he was approached to join the new Vanguard Party which was eventually announced soon after the publication of the White Paper on March 20 the following year, he refused.

He did not agree with the blatant calls for an Independent Ulster and believed it was better to fight from within the party rather than from outside it. He viewed that he was an Ulster Unionist member and was going to remain so. While he understood why Craig felt the need to break away he made it plain he would not go with him – even though he had been a member of the Vanguard pressure group within the party.

The Constitution Bill was debated over several weeks in the spring and summer of 1973 with elections being held for the new Assembly on June 28.

Throughout the debates Molyneaux highlighted what he felt were the "gaping holes" in the legislation. On May 24 he told the House: "On a graver note, an earlier speaker in the debate stated that he thought this Bill was to a great extent a gamble. I would like to leave the House with the thought that the gamble since 1969 has so far cost us 800 lives.

He continued: "Many people believe that Parliament is prepared to gamble, and gamble with lives, because it is not prepared to come down firmly in defence of the integrity of the United Kingdom". He pointed out that he believed the Bill gave too many powers to the Secretary of

State and noted that if the Assembly did not suit them "I suppose in current terminology this would be the unacceptable face of Unionism and the Assembly might be prorogued and even dissolved".

He also condemned proportional representation which was used for the first time in Northern Ireland for the Assembly elections, telling the House on July 3 that he had evidence of a tally room which discovered after two hours voting that people were voting for the first four candidates on the ballot paper who had been a Communist, a true blue Tory Unionist, the SDLP and then the Labour representative. So, he added, there was no possible question of everyone understanding the system.

But the 78 member Assembly was elected and sat under the new Northern Ireland Constitution Act in an attempt to give minorities a greater say in the running of Northern Ireland. There was an apparent lull in political development until November when Faulkner joined in talks with Whitelaw and the SDLP under Gerry Fitt and Alliance under Oliver Napier. The result was the creation of an executive involving the three parties and the pace quickened towards the Sunningdale conference.

However those December talks included the creation of a Council of Ireland and the turmoil within what was rapidly becoming a squabbling, fighting Unionist family spilled over at the Unionist Council meeting on January 4, 1974.

Faulkner went to seek endorsement for the Sunningdale agreement and the power-sharing executive but was heavily defeated. He resigned as Unionist leader three days later but was prepared to go on as chief executive of the new body. Within a matter of weeks Harry West found himself the leader of a party which was falling apart at the seams.

Molyneaux believes Faulkner wasted his talents in allowing himself to join the executive in the full knowledge that it would not work and the majority of Unionists would ensure that it did not. He suggests that the former Prime Minister knew when he arrived at that crucial Council meeting what the outcome would be.

"But I suppose he had gone so far down the road that he felt he could not turn and went on in a lemming kind of fashion."

West holds a similar view remembering his feeling of "total devastation" as Faulkner left the platform that January 4.

"I drove down the road towards Fermanagh, a road I had travelled hundreds and hundreds of times, and I was in a daze. I was very nervous for the future of our country as I had always thought that Faulkner was the man with the ability to see us through the crisis."

But Faulkner resigned as leader on January 7 and West soon found he was elected to the top post on a two to one vote over Molyneaux by the party's standing committee. He accepted it to prevent any further fragmentation of the party as with Faulkner's departure most of the administrative staff in Glengall Street headquarters went too. He also accepted it because no one else wanted it.

Molyneaux confirms that he certainly did not: "There was a view amongst a section within the party that it would be better if they picked somebody who could take a longer view, particularly as they realised the major decisions were now being taken at Westminster. They believed it would have been better to have someone who had Westminster experience and was over there most of the time. My name was put forward.

"But if I am being truthful I did not shed any tears when I was defeated by Harry. Indeed, in many ways, I was relieved and quietly glad."

The beleaguered Executive continued with rows on the floor of the Assembly becoming an every day occurrence. It was placed in an even more uncertain situation when Heath called the famous "Who governs Britain" General Election of February 1974.

This was the chance the anti-Sunningdale Unionists had wanted to prove the strength of opposition there was to the agreement. The election was held on February 28 and the United Ulster Unionist Council, or coalition, took 11 out of the 12 seats. Thanks to a John Laird created slogan "Dublin is just a Sunningdale away", the coalition put up a single candidate in each of the constituencies. Bill Craig took East Belfast from the Faulkner supporter Stanley McMaster as did Robert Bradford from Rafton Pounder in the south of the city. There were other new faces as well, such as Harold McCusker in Armagh and Willie Ross in Londonderry. West won Fermanagh and South Tyrone and the group confidently went to Westminster with the message that the Unionists of Northern Ireland had no confidence in the new administration.

The new Labour Government held a similar, if unstated, view and the support of the UUUC to the Workers' Strike in May was the final blow to the short lived body.

Then came what Secretary of State Merlyn Rees told MPs was a "breathing space" for Northern Ireland before on July 4 he announced another initiative – an elected Constitutional Convention to work out a political settlement.

But his party was facing its own problems at Westminster. The

Wilson administration was a minority one and the Cabinet itself knew it would be short-lived. Parliament was again dissolved on September 10 and a General Election was called for October 10.

This saw the return of a Labour administration with a majority of three and the entrance of Enoch Powell as an Official Unionist MP. The coalition lost one of it seats – Harry West's to Independent Frank Maguire who had stood as an agreed anti-Unionist candidate – and a new Parliamentary leader, James Molyneaux.

During the short Parliament he had been the secretary and whip of the grouping which included Ian Paisley, Bill Craig and Harry West. Because the "Big Three" were very much involved in the Stormont Assembly, Molyneaux had found himself the constant factor in London. The three leaders were flying backwards and forwards to continually attend crisis meetings, while Molyneaux kept the shop at Westminster. It meant that he became the point of reference and was used as an index as to what was going on in Parliament, particularly from an administrative point of view.

He went to the first meeting of the coalition after the election very much aware that they had lost Harry West but in ignorance of what was to happen.

As on previous occasions from his appointment as chairman of the small Diamond branch of the Unionist Party to his nomination as a Unionist candidate, it never struck him that he was going to become the leader of the grouping.

Paisley, Powell and Craig were the three dominant personalities and Molyneaux, as has happened so often in his life, was handed a piece of paper to record the minutes.

"It never dawned on me that there were any concerns about a leader. I assumed we would go back to the previous form of simply having a chairman as in the days of Robin Chichester-Clark and Willie Orr."

As whip he chaired the meeting as well as faithfully recording the minutes on his piece of paper. They expressed their regret at the loss of West and proceeded to nominations for his replacement. Craig's name was proposed and seconded and Powell's was put forward. However he said he would only accept it if it was a unanimous decision, noted that it clearly was not and withdrew. Craig then did likewise and the secretary looked up from his piece of paper when it was decided that he was to be the compromise.

He protested but puts up the guard that he was so thunderstruck by the decision that he just sat there. West maintains he always enjoyed the thought of being leader at Westminster and thrived on the position as he moved towards the overall leadership of the Official Unionist Party.

In spite of being thunderstruck he soon put his foot down about procedures within the grouping. Members began discussing who they should elect for what post within the body.

But the new leader had a different view and said so. The supreme backroom boy told them that he wanted to meet each of them individually and that whilst they might not get the job they would like he would do his best to ensure that talents were put in the right direction.

The reaction? "There was a stunned silence and then Enoch was the first to recover. He clapped his hands and said 'Quite right! What else is a leader for'. I thanked them, stood up and that was the end of the meeting".

This came from the man who said he was a bit overawed by it all.

Unionist commentators have noted that Molyneaux did a worthwhile job during this time as leader simply because, in his own quiet manner, he was able to pull the members together and large personalities like Paisley and Craig were able to work in harmony without trying to outdo one another whilst in Westminster. According to one Molyneaux had a tremendous ability at being able to organise them without too many internal clashes.

One tale of his character, not directly related to his leadership but his "long view" of issues came during a day at Westminster in the mid-Seventies when members of the grouping were issuing statements right, left and centre.

The observer asked Molyneaux as to why he was not doing the same and the South Antrim MP recalled advice proferred by the former Armagh MP Jack Maginnis – Union Jack.

He told the observer that Jack's strategy had been that if such an incident happened and statements were being issued in all directions, his constituents would wonder what the significance was in that he had not followed suit. The tale finished with Molyneaux's customary wry grin.

He enjoyed being the common denominator in the new team. Although they had all been elected in the February poll, apart from Enoch Powell, there really had only been three months at Westminster before the summer recess and an almost immediate dissolution on return.

Molyneaux did speak to them individually about their positions and then found they would seek him out to discuss some political issue. This progressed to constituency issues and then they would make an appointment to come and have a private chat. The appointment meant that it was behind closed doors and no one would barge in half way through on a different matter.

He grew into this role, not in a deliberate manner, but colleagues realised that it was not in his nature to gossip and if something was offered in confidence it would remain so.

This continues today – whether it be from a constituent in Lagan Valley or the Prime Minister. She and he may not have agreed over a certain Anglo-Irish Agreement but confidences have been exchanged and he is regarded highly in Parliament for this characteristic.

He unassumingly puts it this way: "It eventually dawned on me that I was being the common denominator. They trusted me or at least they knew I was not going to go and retell their innermost thoughts to other people. They must have thought too that mug and all as he is, he must have some common sense so his opinion might be worth listening to".

Because of his make-up, because of his long view approach to issues, the burden of other people's problems has not weighed him down. It is not that he takes them lightly but would tend to take them on himself. He sees this as a fault because then, he feels, an objective decision cannot be made and he does his best to divorce himself. That is why many see this cold, rather bland image, never realising that he could have the burdens and worries of 20 people going on inside.

Shortly after Neil Kinnock became Labour leader he and Molyneaux had a meeting. One of Kinnock's first questions was how the older man coped with all the problems his members came to him with. The answer came back that Kinnock should take comfort and strength from this as it proved that his people had accepted him as their leader – a father figure in many ways. The fresh Labour chief replied that the advice would be taken on board and would help in the future.

Molyneaux admits that he does receive comfort from this position: "I would regard myself as a failure if they had to bottle things up and not come to me and talk about it. It would be an indication of failure on my part if I knew that they felt I was so remote that they could not talk to me about their worries".

This is not just confined to the Palace of Westminster. Since becoming party leader the sympathetic ear has extended to constituency associations and rank and file members of the party. The web of conversations and confidences also gives him, in a curious way, a sense of balance when he has to make decisions.

"You see the pressure and influences other people are under and the views they are taking. It is the centre of the spider's web, as you know pretty well what is going on at any given time and you are the only person who does know because by being at the centre you can pull all the threads together."

In his way of chatting to people across Northern Ireland from an Orange Order dinner to a church fete, it actually unwinds him and becomes almost the only hobby he has. It also helps keep a perspective on things because through these conversations he can find his sense of balance. When a scare story comes to him that a certain section of the party in a county is against him, he always knows it is exaggerated as he has spoken to people in the area and understands how they feel.

The leadership role continued to expand at Westminster but he and West got on well, considering the situation was a recipe for misunderstandings and disasters. Molyneaux at the other end of a telephone while West gauged home opinion. Both men agree that the relationship was sound.

"Of course it looked as if it would continually be in trouble. The overall leader based in Belfast while I was leader at Westminster. When you consider that between 1975 and 1979, in spite of the Convention, there was no elected body in the Province I was leading in the only elected tier of government available to Northern Ireland. The possibilities for friction, tension and argument were endless but it did not happen and I believe it was a two way thing. Harry would not pick up on the fine type and was very tolerant while I understood his position, particularly as he had been at Westminster for six months and then lost the seat through no fault of his own."

West's view is that Molyneaux was diligent, was able to use his experience to maximise Unionist influence and did keep him well informed – apart from the infamous 1976 administrative devolution speech.

However he now believes that he did not realise that behind the scenes Molyneaux with supporters such as the Rev Martin Smyth, was undermining him – particularly when Molyneaux was at Westminster and talks of devolution arose.

But an observer who was involved in Unionist politics during the late Seventies maintains he never saw any evidence of Molyneaux being disloyal to the party leader.

He suggests that when Molyneaux disagreed with West he would have argued his case openly in front of others: "He never made any bones about it if it was a policy disagreement. But he certainly never went behind West's back to complain or to drum up a rival camp".

This view is backed by the then party secretary Norman Hutton who, by the very nature of his job, worked closely with both men. He too remembers the policy disagreement but he emphasises that Molyenaux was always very loyal to West.

"In all my dealings with the two men I can never remember Jim Molyneaux doing anything with the deliberate thought of digging away at Harry's position."

The relationship worked on through the heady days of the Callaghan Government and its slim majority when the Unionists found that as a minority party they held, in many instances, the balance of power. The administration struggled on until the Opposition's motion of censure in March 1979 when it was defeated with the help of Northern Ireland MPs Gerry Fitt and Frank Maguire who both abstained.

The first Thatcher Government was elected in May and the following month the United Kingdom faced its first European elections. DUP leader Ian Paisley had a simple message – a straightforward condemnation of the EEC and all that it stood for. But the Official Unionists' had a more muddled approach – they accepted the UK's commitment to membership but called for major changes to meet Northern Ireland's peculiar needs. They also decided to run two candidates, former Stormont Minister John Taylor and the leader.

Paisley was easily elected on the first count in the proportional representation election while SDLP deputy leader John Hume went through on the third. By the fifth count West was eliminated and Taylor went through on the sixth. Northern Ireland's first three MEPs had been selected.

Party officials recognised the drumming it had received, admitted that as many as 100,000 supporters had refused to back the party line and said most had gone for Paisley's outright opposition.

Molyneaux believes West had been ill-advised to stand for selection. Knowing the attitude amongst Unionists towards the EEC, he felt it was wrong that the leader should place his own position in jeopardy. But West felt he had to, particularly with his farming background.

On the second day of the count when it was already clear he would be eliminated, West handed his resignation to Norman Hutton. The party secretary knew what it was and for a fortnight tried, with the other party officers, to persuade him not to go.

However West who, by this time, was tired of what he felt was the internal party sore of devolution versus integration felt it was the only honourable thing to do. Among those who tried to talk him out of his decision was a party vice-president Jim Molyneaux.

"Everyone on the officers' team did their best to implore him not to go. We were coming into the summer lull and everyone in the Province was tired of elections, we had just had both a Westminster and an EEC poll, and no one in the party wanted to face such an internal one. We knew everyone's attention would be focused on the new administration in the autumn and before long it would have been the party council's annual meeting. I am convinced that members would have been in no mood for a change and the arrangement would have gone on as it was.

"I kept telling him to hold on and simply let the water flow under the bridge but he was determined to go."

The officers' implorings fell on stony ground and West formally tendered his resignation at an officers' meeting in early July. He also received the support of the officers when he suggested that Molyneaux take on a caretaking role until a special meeting of the council could be held in the autumn.

The Westminster leader took on the responsibilities immediately. Primarily, he claims, because West suggested it himself but also because there was the fear that the party was still not in a fit state of health and leaderless, its support would fall away again in the constituency associations.

West, however, believes this gave Molyneaux the opportunity he had been waiting to try out the role for size and made statements during the caretaking period which he had no right to do.

"It was a bold thing to do as he had not been formally elected as leader yet he was making speeches, particularly on devolution, as if he was speaking on behalf of the party."

The special Council meeting took place in the Ulster Hall in Belfast in early September. Contenders were Robert Bradford and Austin Ardill. The result was a foregone conclusion – Ardill came a poor third and Molyneaux beat Bradford by a three to one majority.

The supreme backroom boy and organiser had made it to the top of the pile. But again it did not show. The face remained in neutral, while inside he could not help but feel slightly amused by it all.

One observer notes: "In a sense it is a great tribute to him that a man of his shy nature and background should have coped with being leader, first of all of a very diverse grouping at Westminster and secondly the largest party in Northern Ireland".

But his former leader thinks he is really a very small man – both physically and mentally as well as being very narrow minded.

"He has been a great disappointment to me," is how Harry West sums up Jim Molyneaux.

Shortly after Molyneaux became the elected leader, as is tradition, it is understood he put West's name forward for an honour. A suggestion came back and was put to West who refused. The reason? It is believed because it was not high enough up the honours' ladder – it was not a "Lordship".

5.   Broad Church

Within weeks of his becoming leader, Molyneaux had to make his first major policy decision. He had hardly time to survey his own party and analyse its state of health, before he was faced with the Atkins round table conference.

The Conservatives had swept to power that May of 1979 and Humphrey Atkins, the party's chief whip, had been appointed to the Northern Ireland bed of nails – the job the late Airey Neave was to have filled. It had been Neave, with Molyneaux's help and advice, who had drawn up the regional council, administrative devolution policy spelt out in the Conservative manifesto for the General Election.

It had said that "in the absence of devolved government, we will seek to establish one or more elected regional councils with a wide range of powers over local services."

The new Ulster Unionist leader had high hopes that in spite of the loss of Neave, Atkins would take up the policy and carry it through. Soon after his appointment at Stormont Castle, the new Secretary of State and the Unionist chief met and had their usual cordial conversation.

Molyneaux still presumed that the policy would be implemented – even if on an extended timetable. During the March crisis which had seen the fall of the Callaghan Government, Molyneaux had made certain with Neave, just a few days before his murder, that an advisory commission would be set up to see how the policy would be applied.

He had not wanted a Royal Commission as it would have taken up to 18 months and the whole object, as far as he was concerned, was to get rid of direct rule and start the process of restoring devolved power to a regional assembly or council in Northern Ireland.

This had been agreed by Thatcher, Neave and the Unionist leader during the previous year when the manifesto was being drawn up. The Commission of experts would have decided what legislative changes were needed so that the new body could have transferred subjects and Northern Ireland, Molyneaux hoped, would have been on the road to devolution.

But there was a distinct cooling in relationships between Molyneaux and the fresh Secretary of State after the summer recess of 1979 and he did not realise, in spite of his long view, that the plans for a conference were well underway.

The Secretary of State told the House of Commons on October 25, 1979, that his talks with party leaders in Northern Ireland had confirmed the Government's view that it was right to transfer back to locally elected representatives some "at least of the powers of government at present exercised from Westminster".

"It will", he told members, "in due course be a matter for Parliament to decide on proposals put to it by the Government, what kind of powers and responsibilities are to be transferred to elected representatives of the people of Northern Ireland and through what kind of institutions they are to be exercised. The Government wish, however, to put forward proposals that, so far as possible, have the agreement of the people of Northern Ireland".

A consultative document was to serve as a basis of the conference and this set out the range of powers and responsibilities the Government was prepared to hand out to the Northern Ireland representatives. It also stated what the Government regarded as "reasonable and appropriate" arrangements to take account of the interests of the minority.

Atkins continued: "Our aim will be to secure from the conference, drawing on the suggestions in the consultative document workable and acceptable arrangements for restoring to the people of Northern Ireland greater responsibility for the conduct of their own affairs which we can then recommend to this House in the fulfilment of our commitment in the Queen's Speech".

However Molyneaux bluntly told him: "Does the Secretary of State recall that I have constantly made clear to him, privately and publicly, that the Ulster Unionist Party will not engage in time-wasting exercises and window dressing of that type? Is he also aware that we shall, however, carefully and reasonably consider, in the Northern Ireland Committee or on the floor of the House, any proposals brought forward to give effect to the specific suggestions and commitments in the Conservative manifesto".

The Secretary of State of course rejected this but admitted that he was aware that the member for Antrim South was anxious to move in a broad direction which was "naturally" going to be one of the directions the Government was seeking for "the agreement of everyone who wants it".

But there were questions being raised even from the Conservative backbenches on the Government's sincerity. The Peterborough MP Dr Brian Mawhinney expressed his disappointment at the Government's proposals and suggested that an increasing number of people believed that the determination of successive Governments to have talks, and talks about talks, was understood by many "to be a rationale for doing nothing or, even worse, a reason for not knowing what to do".

The consultative paper appeared on November 20 and was entitled "The Government of Northern Ireland – A Working Paper for a Conference". As well as setting out ways in which powers could be transferred, it also suggested a number of ways minority interests could be safeguarded – including weighted votes in an assembly to give the minority some blocking powers.

But on top of the Molyneaux rejection of the plans, came the SDLP's who maintained there had to be an Irish dimension. It was not only thrown out by its constituency representatives but by its executive as well, forcing Gerry Fitt to resign as leader and utter the fear that a "republican element was emerging within the ranks of the SDLP".

In spite of the rancour the conference eventually met at Stormont on January 7, 1980 with the DUP, SDLP and the Alliance Party in attendance. The largest party in Northern Ireland did not change its view – it had decided to boycott the proceedings and that was it. To Molyneaux it was a point of principle. There was no need for such talks, the Conservative manifesto set out clearly the creation of a regional council and that district councils would receive more powers. The Secretary of State simply had to set up a Commission to see how this policy could be implemented.

In many ways this was a brash stand by the fledgling party leader. In spite of being chief at Westminster he had not had time to gauge the overall mood of the party to the conference. There was still the shadow of West hanging over him and the immediate comparisons were rife amongst party members from headquarters staff down. Flamboyant farmer replaced by deadpan workaholic.

But, as when he informed his Parliamentary colleagues that he, and no one else, would appoint them to their spokesmen positions, Molyneaux dug his heels in and flatly refused to attend the Stormont gathering. He simply felt it was a betrayal of all he had quietly and steadily worked for. It was, for him, a complete about-turn on what had been set out in the Conservative manifesto on Northern Ireland – the very section he had helped Airey Neave formulate. However his former leader feels it was the greatest political mistake ever made by the Ulster

Unionist Party and the responsibility for it rests on Molyneaux's shoulders.

West tried to warn the new chief of the dangers of boycotting the conference but these were ignored. West points out that no one knew what was on offer until discussions got underway and then the Ulster Unionists had no input.

"When the talks began we found that one of the alternatives which was on offer was a majority government with safeguards for the minority. That was exactly what we had been fighting for in the Convention", he states.

"To my amazement Molyneaux was allowed by the party to boycott that conference and we remained out in the cold."

The then Secretary of State also expresses regret over Molyneaux's decision but takes a different view on what had been planned by the Government: "It is quite true that the election manifesto of our party in 1979 was very clear that some kind of administrative devolution was very important and that this could take several forms, one of which might be the establishment of two or more regional councils. That was not the only suggestion but it certainly was one of them.

"It was with that objective in mind that I started discussions with all the parties. However it became clear to me very quickly indeed that what mattered was not so much the precise form of the government, be it local, regional or Province-wide, as to how its power was going to be administered. It did not matter if you were talking about a 'reborn Stormont' or regional councils or local councils. The one question which had to be solved before anything else could be moved forward, was how was power to be exercised.

"That was where the great divide between the Unionists and the minority parties' view existed. It was in order to see whether there was any way in which that void could be bridged that I thought it right to get all the parties together. It was a great pity that Jim Molyneaux and his party did not come as we missed their guidance and wisdom and as a result the conference was inconclusive."

Lord Colnbrook believes it was short-sighted on Molyneaux's part to decide not to attend as his aim was exactly the same as the Unionist leader's – the establishment of a devolved administration in Northern Ireland.

"The pity about it which came to me immediately was that here were the various political parties and the different points of view actually sitting down and talking to each other. There were a lot of people who told me that they reckoned the round table conference would last 20 minutes – in fact it lasted three months.

The fact that these different points of view could be aired, calmly and without rancour and without anybody losing their temper, I think was helpful. It did not, I know, produce a solution but the actual physical act of sitting down around a table and trying to thrash it out, I think was beneficial to everyone."

But he claims it was not beneficial to the Ulster Unionists and emphasises that it was sad that they were not there. West backs this up and describes Molyneaux's decision as a "very great tragedy". He firmly believes that if progress could have been made then more than five years later the Anglo-Irish Agreement would not have been imposed.

The subfusc leader believed then and has not changed his opinion since, that a country cannot have a system of government where one named party be always considered for a certain number of seats on an executive. To do so, he believes, is handing one party a veto over a majority which it has no right to. He laughs at times when he is described as the moderate Unionist leader in comparison to Ian Paisley when he has always said he will not become involved in any power-sharing body. How he couches his opinion tends to make him sound more conciliatory than he really is.

There has, however, always been his recognition that the "halcyon" days of Stormont would never return and began, in 1976, to try and make his party realise that it was an opposition party and not a "government in waiting". When he became leader he adopted this as a central theme, believing that the "acceptance of that reality was a necessary prerequisite to future success at any level". He will never forgive Ted Heath – not for abolishing Stormont but for what he considers a greater crime, not replacing it with some form of administration other than direct rule.

So in his own quiet, cautious way, when he began his term of office he started to apply his long view again on how the party would become a "broad church" and represent as many strands of Unionism as possible. The Unionist Coalition had disintegrated three years earlier when Bill Craig had suggested that there should be a voluntary coalition which would have included the SDLP. He was expelled from the coalition and Ernest Baird and others in Vanguard who opposed Craig's view, created the U.U.U. Movement. It left itself with little power and support and the final collapse came when the Coalition's steering committee formed a United Unionist Action Council which took in paramilitary groups and backed the abortive loyalist strike of 1977. The Official Unionist leader Harry West said he could not support such a

venture and the ramifications moved on to Westminster where the
coalition fell apart. Ian Paisley and John Dunlop had supported the
failed stoppage.

Because of Molyneaux's decision not to enter the Atkins' talks the
now rapidly maturing chestnut that he was an integrationist and not a
"proper" devolutionist meant more confusion in the ranks. When he
surveyed the party in late 1979 the devolution lobby was very vocal and
in the first few months of his leadership service he faced severe criticism
of his handling of what others viewed as a fresh political initiative from
the Government. The strands of Unionism were all there but they were
not weaving together. He recognised the hard work West had put into
rescuing the party from the brink of collapse. Now he wanted to build
on those foundations.

"There had been so many splinter groups during the early and
mid-seventies that it was time for a period of quiet, steady consolidation. Simple, plain hard work was needed to show that the Unionist
party could be a broad church and while sections could hold differing
views on parts of party policy they would back the overall package."

The officer team of the party backed his stand on the Atkins talks but
he had to cope with a barrage of criticism from the devolution lobby.

"There was a section of Unionism both within and without the party
which opposed my line. When they were not making any dent in my
determination, they then resorted to the allegation that I would not go
to the conference because I did not want devolution. It was utterly
untrue. I could see from the beginning that the Atkins initiative could
not possibly result in the establishment of a devolved government and I
was vindicated within three months when the conference fell apart
simply because no agreement was possible.

"If our party had been there, there would have been even more
disagreement in a sense because we would have taken a firm stand on
the constitution and we would have voiced our opposition to power-
sharing. My objection to power-sharing is not that I would not want the
minority represented in government. My main objection then and still
is that it is unworkable. Even Margaret Thatcher and Charles Haughey
agree on that. The type of power-sharing the Northern Ireland Office
was attempting to force on us does not exist anywhere else in the world.
Coalitions exist and fall apart and a further one is created in its place.
Whereas in Northern Ireland it was to be a compulsory, permanent
coalition which was unworkable."

He was confident that his view would prevail. He had been elected
just a few months earlier by a vast majority so he had an inner fortitude

that once he had explained what could or, more relatively, could not be achieved through the conference, then the party knew where it stood with him.

However a major differing view on how Northern Ireland should be governed came from the former Conservative Cabinet Minister and then MP for Down South, Enoch Powell. He advocated complete integration with the rest of the United Kingdom and repeated his opinion at every opportunity – much to the annoyance of the main-stream of the party.

Speculation as to how Powell has influenced Molyneaux and subsequently party policy over the years, has always been rife. The towering intellectual with the public elementary side-kick. Former Secretary of State Jim Prior describes the relationship as being like a rabbit transfixed by a stoat.

It began in the early seventies before Powell left the Conservative Party. In 1972, a few weeks after the second reading of the European Communities Bill and the abolition of Stormont, Powell came to Molyneaux and asked if he could spare him half an hour of his time. This puzzled the backbencher in that a man of national standing had sought him out and asked him if he had time to spare for a private chat. They had met before at Unionist rallies in Northern Ireland but had only been on polite speaking terms.

However Molyneaux, along with Armagh MP Jack Maginnis, had been the two Unionist MPs to voice their strong opposition to member-ship of the European Community. The meeting subsequently took place and Powell informed the backbencher that a person with integrity could only survive in the House of Commons if he had a cause for which to fight. He said he had two – opposition to the EEC and a second, Northern Ireland. With that he informed Molyneaux that he under-stood how Unionists felt with the imposition of direct rule and if he could be of any help then he was at the backbencher's disposal. It was a short, crisp meeting of a type which suited, and still does, both men.

It was not repeated and Molyneaux rejects the suggestion that Powell was a carpetbagger and that, after he left the Conservative Party, he decided to look around for a peg on which to hang his superior political hat and found the Unionist Party.

"I feel I cannot accept that point of view at all as that meeting two years even before Enoch left the Conservative Party proves the point that he was already willing to serve Northern Ireland and the Unionist cause."

Powell was adopted as the Ulster Unionist candidate in South Down

on August 30, 1974, after a packed meeting in Dromore Orange Hall,
Four months earlier the Big Three of West, Paisley and Craig had
visited the daunting figure in his London home to confirm his availabi-
lity for a candidacy as a Unionist. The three leaders were enthusiastic at
the thought of having such a national figure coming to the aid of the
Unionist cause. Particularly Paisley.

Captain Willie Orr secured the South Down seat in the February
election but by early autumn he had decided, for personal reasons, not
to stand again. However until Capt. Orr made this decision there
literally was no room at the inn for Powell. There had been vague
suggestions that others within the coalition would not be seeking
re-selection but these remained ill-defined.

The South Antrim member decided on another plan. Because there
was no clear slot in which to place Prophet Powell, he decided that he
would tender his resignation. He consulted his constituency chairman
Joe Cunningham who was not greatly amused and when he put the
suggestion to Powell the offer was flatly rejected.

"I had been there for four frustrating years, I could see that Heath
had been within an ace of breaking the Unionist mould as he had set out
to do. At that stage he might still have succeeded in doing so and Enoch
was one of the few men who could stop him. I thought he had a more
valuable contribution to make than I had. It was as simple as that. It was
not an unselfish gesture. I plainly recognised that he had greater
abilities than I had and would be a great strengthening of the Unionist
team."

The leaders soon had the chance of putting Powell before the
electorate. The United Kingdom went to the polls for the second time
in 1974 on October 10 in a bid by the Wilson Government to gain a
majority in the Commons. Powell was returned in South Down by
3,567 votes. There was no change in any of the other Northern Ireland
seats apart from the loss of Harry West in Fermanagh.

In Patrick Cosgrave's The Lives of Enoch Powell, the author describes the new Unionist leader at Westminster as a "man of few words",
however "what began as a necessary alliance ripened into friendship
and comradeship. Powell and Molyneaux exactly complemented one
another as to character. Powell could always provide the arguments and
the eloquence. Molyneaux could always provide the down to earth
wisdom of an Ulster farmer".

Former Labour leader Michael Foot agrees. He does not believe
Molyneaux has been dominated by Powell to the detriment of the
Unionist cause at Westminster.

"In his own right, he has made himself into a very considerable Parliamentarian. I have nothing but admiration for the way he has handled a very difficult job. Of course Enoch influenced and coached him on procedures and so on in the House but I know that when Jim Molyneaux speaks he speaks as himself, not as someone else's puppet."

However Lord Prior maintains Molyneaux has always been misled by Powell into believing that integration is the answer to the Ulster problem: "He has always appeared to believe that once you got integration then you would remove for all time any chance of the Republic demanding a say in the affairs of Northern Ireland. An attitude of 'well, if this is done then they will go away' which is simply not realistic.

"But while I do point that out and what I believe has been the very marked influence of Enoch, it does not take away from my view that Jim Molyneaux has served his community at all times to the best of his ability and at considerable personal danger. He has always shown a great deal of courage."

Powell still receives a weekly telephone call from the Unionist leader to keep him informed of the day to day situation – both at Parliament and in Northern Ireland. He thinks Molyneaux has always had one major advantage over his Unionist colleagues – he understands the English mentality – something which stemmed from his wartime experiences.

"When an Englishman is angry he becomes silent, when an Ulsterman is angry he shouts. Jim understands both exactly, he can bridge the Irish Sea like no other Ulster politician. It is his unique talent."

This, according to Powell, has helped him in his work at Westminster. He is also adamant that in spite of the popular view, he has always accepted Molyneaux's judgement on how best to serve the Unionist cause.

"It would be true to say that I have never made a speech of which the text has not been previously read by Jim Molyneaux." This is probably why the integration/devolution debate continues to rumble on in the Ulster Unionist Party.

Molyneaux believed that expressing such views was healthy for the party. He recognised that Powell, as a prominent member, had a right to put forward his opinions. In contrast, while the South Down MP advocated total integration, the MP for Londonderry and now East Londonderry, Willie Ross, put forward the case for immediate devolution.

"I saw no reason to stifle the debate. Willie came to me on several occasions to seek my views on his speeches and when he asked if there was conflict with Enoch, I said 'yes but that is the stuff of politics'. Provided there was nothing which was going to be damaging to the party or nothing which was going to be manifestly opposite to the thrust of general party policy then they had their own freedom."

He saw his job, if he was asked to vet any speech from a member of the Parliamentary team, as one which ensured that there was no blatant contradiction to party policy.

He also recognised the logic of Powell's speeches when he continually repeated that Northern Ireland should be governed as an integral part of the United Kingdom. He remembers an incident from his youth which illustrates this point: "How could I condemn Enoch for saying this when I had stood on the lawn at Langford Lodge and had heard Craigavon emphasise that his policy was to ensure that Northern Ireland would remain an integral part of the United Kingdom. There was a Prime Minister of a devolved government pointing out that it was an integral part of the kingdom and who recognised that when it came to a conflict between the sovereign Parliament and the Stormont Government that the Stormont administration had to back down. They made no fuss about it and even though some Cabinet members always gave an air of being equal, in reality they backed down because they realised Westminster was the sovereign power".

The former leader Harry West recognised the need for such a figure as Powell at that critical time in 1974 but he frankly points out that the former Cabinet Minister became a problem when he began to make his integration speeches.

"However having said that at least Powell was honest and made it clear in each speech that his views were not party policy and that he was expressing his own opinions."

The internal wranglings on policy were put very markedly on display during the Atkins' conference boycott period. Clifford Smyth in his book "Ian Paisley, Voice of Protestant Ulster" notes that Molyneaux's decision had a knock on effect in that it pushed the DUP closer to the centre of Ulster politics. Paisley attended, although was not involved in the parallel talks with the SDLP on its "Irish dimension".

He also suggests that any advantage gained by the Official Unionists' outflanking the DUP on the conference which petered out in March 1980, disappeared because of the party's "inability to curtail public wrangling between its spokesmen over party policy. One faction privately agreed with the integration line of Powell but another vociferous faction pressed the case for devolution".

The emergence of the DUP as a major fact of political life in Northern Ireland was another cold cloth to Molyneaux's new leadership. As well as attempting to build on the process begun by Harry West to re-establish the Glengall Street party after its fragmentation in the middle Seventies, Molyneaux also had to face the rivalry for the Unionist vote.

The glaring example of this was obviously Paisley's massive vote in the first European election. It had been another knock in the teeth for the old party, after it had just begun to gather its senses again. Its senior members had to recognise that many of their traditional voters had flocked to Paisley so that he could rightly say he was the voice of Ulster in Europe and that his vote had been a "twentieth century miracle".

The establishment of an alternative, more militant brand of Union-ism had also been evident in the 1979 General Election when Peter Robinson won the East Belfast seat from Bill Craig and Johnny McQuade took North Belfast over Cecil Walker for the Glengall Street party. The Ulster Unionist predicament was compounded by the defection of Jim Kilfedder who stood as an Independent in his old constituency of North Down and won easily with a 23,625 majority.

So throughout the Atkins debate Molyneaux not only had to attempt to marry the Ulster parochial attitude that some day Stormont would return to Powell's fervent belief in the Union through integration but was also forced to look over his shoulder at the swelling support for the DUP. It resulted in what many then and still do regard as his am-bivalence towards party policy – privately for integration, publicly seeking, now and then, devolution. In actual fact the man's primary aim was and has been since, to ensure the survival of a party which was dead apart from the burial in the mid-Seventies.

By doing so, brick by brick, he has felt it is one way of ensuring the continuation of the Union – election results tell successive Govern-ments that the foundation and walls of Unionism will not go away. The roof may fly off now and then but the walls remain.

The growing support for the DUP continued and in December 1980 was given an even greater boost by London and Dublin. Margaret Thatcher and the Irish Prime Minister Charles Haughey met to discuss "the totality of relationships within these islands". While Molyneaux tried to issue reasoned, calm objections Paisley simply declared it was a betrayal. During the late winter and early spring of the following year the Big Man went on the Carson Trail. He was first found by a group of reporters half way up a hill outside Ballymena. The small band had been carefully ushered to the stage managed site to see 500 men wave firearm certificates in the air. They were told it was only a sample of the resistance the Prime Minister would face if the Dublin talks continued. Meanwhile Molyneaux was still looking at the plans for his broad church party.

The different approaches were reflected in the local government elections of May 20, 1981. The DUP was still making the running for the Unionist vote. It gained 26.7 per cent of the poll and for the first time in its ten year history had members in each of Northern Ireland's 26 council chambers. This was regarded as the wayward Unionist child becoming an even more strident adult.

The momentum continued when on November 14 Robert Bradford was shot dead outside his constituency clinic in Finaghy. While Molyneaux tried to keep the troops together and ensure, once again, that they did not fall apart, Paisley, Robinson and McQuade were suspended from the House of Commons for interruptions during a short debate on the murder of a member of the House.

At a Press conference a few hours later Paisley and his colleagues declared that they had no other option but to call on the people of Northern Ireland to make it impossible for the Prime Minister and her Ministers to govern the Province. Bradford, of course, had been an Ulster Unionist member but again Paisley had grabbed the headlines and had left Molyneaux standing in the shadow mourning the loss of a colleague.

The day of action took place on November 23 when memorial services were held throughout Northern Ireland and work stopped. Molyneaux, as outlined in another chapter, attended three and kept well out of the media limelight.

However in spite of Paisley's apparent indomitable profile at this time, his party was unable to further enhance its gains on the Official Unionists. The by-election to fill the vacant South Belfast seat took place on March 4, 1982 and two clerics waged for the spoils – Martin Smyth for the Official Unionists, the Rev William McCrea for the DUP. Because of the successive gains made by Paisley's party, the DUP was in a confident mood. But Smyth was returned by a majority of 5,397. The DUP support had peaked and, in many ways, has not regained the momentum.

Another initiative for Northern Ireland was being hatched. The Secretary of State Jim Prior who had received a hostile, aggressive and undignified reception at Robert Bradford's funeral in Dundonald, was beginning talks on what eventually became his Devolution Bill.

Relations between Molyneaux and Prior during the new Secretary of

State's first few months were cordial. They met on several occasions on a one to one basis and it was during one of these meetings that Prior told Molyneaux that he had been coming round to his way of thinking on power-sharing. He informed the Unionist leader that he felt he knew how devolution could be achieved without incorporating power-sharing. With this at the back of his mind Molyneaux organised a party team, made up from members of the executive including Harold McCusker, the late Michael Armstrong and Sir George Clarke, to have exploratory talks with the Ulster Secretary.

The first couple of meetings went well but, as with the Atkins process, Prior began to change direction at the third gathering.

"He had hardened up his views and said he wanted a cross community consent clause. When we asked him what that meant he informed us that a government could not be run in Northern Ireland unless the entire community supported it. I, of course, said you mean power-sharing to which I got the reply 'well, you do not have to call it that'."

Relations deteriorated from then on. The fourth meeting confirmed the Unionist team's worst fears – a 70 per cent approval both inside and outside the envisaged assembly had to be achieved before power would be returned to a certain area of administration in Northern Ireland.

Sir George Clarke asked the Secretary of State what would happen if the SDLP did not approve of a certain piece of legislation and withdrew its consent. He was bluntly told that if that happened then Prior would be forced to claw back any powers which had been devolved. The senior Unionist figure informed the Secretary of State that the team would leave the meeting in a state of depression and would probably not return. He was correct, the party executive rejected the Prior proposals and the team never did go back to Stormont.

In spite of this the Bill went through its various Parliamentary stages with the Unionists voting against it. The member for Down South viewed it as a facet of a conspiracy between top civil servants in London and Dublin. It was, he maintained, an attempt to detach Northern Ireland from the rest of the UK. By stating this Powell was reflecting the views held by both the party executive and its MPs.

The Ulster Unionist team went reluctantly to the Stormont Assembly as Molyneaux began to witness a growing animosity between Powell and Paisley. Cosgrave highlights that Powell was suspicious of, and often openly hostile to Paisley. The difficulty, according to the author, that Powell faced was that it was seldom easy to work out exactly where Paisley stood or in what direction he was going. This did not suit Powell who was continuing his advocacy of complete administrative integration.

He attacked Paisley at every opportunity believing his Unionism was always conditional and hated his flirtations with an independent Ulster course.

In one speech in Donaghadee he noted: "There is no other party (Ulster Unionist) in Ulster which is the party of the Union, no other party which puts first, before all other considerations, the Union and the maintenance of the Union and which sets its face against anything which might endanger or question or qualify the Union. Others insert the word 'Unionist' in their description, as the crow in the fable strutted around in borrowed feathers; but their profession of being Unionists will not survive an examination of their words and actions".

Powell also declared on more than one occasion that devolution was dead. Once again making Molyneaux's life as leader of a party which had always advocated such a state of constitutional affairs, uneasy. But again Molyneaux believed his colleague had a right to say it as long as he made it plain he was reflecting his own views, not the entire party.

In another blatant attack on Paisley, in spite of words of caution from Molyneaux, Powell, commenting on the Prior initiative, said: "A leading role in the whole business has been played by the Democratic Unionist Party, and its leader Ian Paisley, who was deeply involved in the scheme to assure the Province and the world, in tones somewhat above a whisper, that the new show should have been in operation by now – exactly what Ministers and officials in the Northern Ireland Office were counting upon. It is not the first of the Reverend Doctor's predictions to go amiss. It was also not the first, nor the last, occasion on which he was to reveal himself as the most resourceful, inveterate, and powerful enemy of the Union".

Such utterings brought Paisley's wrath down on the Unionist MP for South Down with descriptions such as "foreigner and Anglo-Catholic" being mounted against Powell. Paisley also decided that the seat would be contested at the first opportunity.

In the meantime the "new show", as described by Powell, got underway. The 78 member Assembly election took place on October 20, 1982, and in spite of its known opposition the Glengall Street party kept the DUP at bay. Paisley's party did not match its previous year's triumphs in the local government elections and its percentages dropped to 22.9 per cent of the poll. The SDLP boycotted the Assembly from the beginning, maintaining there had to be an Irish dimension within its perimeter. Boycott became the trade-mark of the Stormont gathering.

While the DUP worked hard on its committees which monitored the various Government departments, the ambivalent Official Unionist view continued. Molyneaux carried out his duties but remained detached, preferring to cross his legs and stare into space from the front bench. He was also able to quell what appeared to be several rumblings of rebellions from within his own team. For a time it seemed that Harold McCusker was everybody's darling and was being pushed forward as a much better spokesman for the Ulster Unionists in the body than the leader. This precipitated press speculation that Molyneaux's reign was coming to an end and that his authority was continually being undermined.

The "long view" came into play again. He could see that because of the party's disapproval of the initiative, the "dirty tricks" brigade from "on high" would begin its operation. He recalls a press conference when the speculation was rife that his position was untenable. He was asked if the rumoured plots to remove him were undermining his own confidence.

The reply was: "No, I do not feel greatly disturbed by them. I hope anybody who is engaged in that type of activity will realise that I am not going to go quietly. There will be blood on the floor and they will have to have strong stomachs".

He pointed out that he was elected by the Ulster Unionist Council and if it decided that it wanted rid of him then he would obey. He added: "I am not going to be pushed off the cliff by some caucus". That ended the rebellion.

Meanwhile in spite of the DUP's hard Assembly work it gave Paisley's party little reward in the General Election of June 1983 – including the failure to grasp Powell's seat. It was the first time Northern Ireland went to the polls to select 17 MPs rather than 12.

Molyneaux's own constituency of South Antrim, the largest in the UK, was split up, part of Newtownabbey, including the massive Rathcoole estate, went to East Antrim and the south of the constituency became known as Lagan Valley. DUP defector Roy Beggs stood in East Antrim, Clifford Forsythe, a well-liked but unknown constituency worker, stood in the reduced South Antrim, while the party leader went to Lagan Valley. Tactically it proved better than the party had hoped for. Paisley remained in North Antrim while party stalwart and rising star Jim Allister went to do battle in East Antrim. Beggs squeezed past the post in the new constituency.

Armagh was divided into Upper Bann and Newry/Armagh and the Glengall Street party gained both. The two parties had agreed that they would not split the Unionist vote in three constituencies, hence the Official Unionist gain in Newry/Armagh. Ken Maginnis was returned in Fermanagh and Mid-Ulster was clinched by DUP man William McCrea. But his gain was cancelled out by the Official Unionist victory of Cecil Walker in North Belfast.

South Down was keenly viewed by the public and press. Paisley put forward candidate Cecil Harvey, a well known party member with a base in the constituency. Meanwhile Powell also had to contend with a reduced constituency from 97,000 to 69,000 and most of the areas he lost were predominantly Unionist. According to Cosgrave, Powell predicted to his wife that he would win by 500 votes, he did by 550 over the SDLP's Eddie McGrady. Paisley's attempt to put Powell, the man he had so earnestly sought to bring into Unionist politics, in his place had failed dismally. Harvey had only gained 3,743 and had lost his deposit in the process.

Molyneaux has seen the party win 11 out of the 17 seats he had battled for at Westminster. His long view of the "broad church" was becoming a reality. He had witnessed the disintegration of the party in the mid-Seventies. Rather than leave with Bill Craig he had decided to stay with "the old firm" and restore the party to what he regarded as one of its main principles – power in the hands of the constituency associations, rather than those of the leader as Faulkner thought he had.

It helps to realise that he is the first Unionist leader who has come up through the ranks and, at times, does not receive enough credit for achieving this. He would never say it himself. Gone is the "big house" dominance of the Glengall Street party. Molyneaux saw his way through all administrative aspects of it which has given him a sound background in his leadership role.

However there remains the residue of the days gone by and the snobbery. Even Jim Prior, an Englishman looking into the Northern Ireland society structure, noted how sarcastically the Unionist aristocracy treated Molyneaux. In his conversations with them they pointed out that Molyneaux was only a farmer's son and one with no background – it might stretch back to Norman sheep farmers but that did not matter. This Prior felt was very cruel and unfair to the man.

Molyneaux, having no airs about himself, pays no attention to such jibes. They never do hurt him. He prefers to make sure that he helps, as best he can, the people "on the ground" in the party. His work through the ranks means that people know he understands and that they do not have to spend half an hour trying to explain something to him.

"It is because you know what the problems are in a given electoral ward and what that means in the running of an election that you know what the people are facing and you can relate to their problems immediately. I suppose what is even more important is that because they know that you did come up through the ranks, you did go through that mill that they know you do understand. That has a curious effect because if they do come to you with a problem, they know that you are already sympathetic and that you will do your best to help them overcome that particular problem."

He does believe there is more power now back with the constituency associations than there has been since the party's "break-down" in the Seventies.

"It is good to know that the responsibility is back with them in playing their part in the shaping of policy. When Stormont was around the party organisation played only a limited part in the projection of policy. There was no day to day feed-in simply because the Cabinet was making the decisions. While it and the officers' team did mesh together at times, there was no unitary structure. I would like to think that now the executive and the officers' team are far more alive, both in a political and administrative sense. It makes for a much healthier party.

Molyneaux believes too that by allowing the different strands to air their views in public and against press criticism that it has made them more unified in remaining Ulster Unionist.

"I would like to think that that is the position today. We have hundreds of people in the party who would have been strong backers of Terence O'Neill, Chichester Clarke and Faulkner, indeed some of those who went with Brian to form the Unionist Party of Northern Ireland. But they are all in our fold now and they all have their say. It is a broad church and I believe it is the healthiest way for the party to continue.

"Because I believe if we were not like that, then we could not have mustered the force we did, in the political sense, against the Anglo-Irish Agreement. There would have been some, out on a wing, saying maybe we had better co-operate, while there would have been others who were maintaining it would be gone in a week. That was not the collective attitude. They had the feeling, we are going to stick together, we do not like this, we are going to resist it as best we can and that, broadly, remains the position. We could not have done that ten years ago.

"If I had not taken that long view all those years ago I do not think it would have been possible to have mustered them all together and to have held them together after a fashion."

It returns to his old before one's time characteristic. The long view had been helped by his insight into the aftermath administration of the war.

"Montgomery was the Commander in Chief of the British zone in Germany. He was inclined not be a unifier but was very abrasive and trod on people's toes. While the staff work was alright, mainly because his staff were good, when he became Chief of the Imperial General Staff it was something of a disaster, simply because he was not a unifier.

"Seeing somebody close up like that left an impression on me. By seeing and realising how defective it could be was a warning to me not to go down the same path. Not that I was ever contemplating being in that kind of position but somehow it brushes off on you. For your own little part in occupied Germany you were trying to do something for the best on the administrative side. Then a certain directive would arrive which would cause an unholy war whereas if it had been drafted in another way and explained properly, its primary aim would have been achieved without a row and the subsequent repercussions."

In his modest manner he does not suggest that the success of 1983 has been the achievement of his primary objective since he became leader. He views the Anglo-Irish Agreement as another attempt to splinter Unionism.

However in early 1989 he sent a subtle reminder to the press and media. He pointed out that it was incorrect to describe the Glengall Street party, in reports, as Official Unionist. The accurate description, he declared, was the Ulster Unionist Party. He obviously felt confident enough that the party had regained its self-esteem and the variety of strands had, after several years, been woven together. A game of patience had been won.

6. Westminster

Jim Molyneaux has a flat in London's South Kensington – the inside of which he rarely sees. It is used more often by family and friends who are either holidaying in the capital or are in transit. The door is always open, a request to use the accommodation rarely turned down and as long as the guest does not get in the owner's way when he is making his breakfast there is no disharmony. And in spite of his bachelor status and his County Antrim origins, he is generous to a fault.

Former party secretary Norman Hutton and his wife Doris stayed in the flat when they attended a Buckingham Palace garden party. Not only was the accommodation made readily available but an envelope was left on the living room table. There is no need to say what was inside as with so many acts of kindness on Molyneaux's part, they are never disclosed to the outside world. Only those who are at the receiving end thank him and remember. They too never boast.

Molyneaux rarely sees the inside of the flat because he is usually at another House. This initiates many on this side of the Irish Sea to often repeat "the wee man is never around when you want him". He is, however, at the other end of a telephone and, as he points out himself, is easier to find at the House of Commons than when he is in Northern Ireland because he is usually either carrying out constituency work or attending functions.

He was irritated once to discover that a broadcasting organisation, to which everyone is supposed to make a financial contribution, had learnt of his flat number. He was not annoyed that they would disturb him during the small hours of a morning. What concerned him most was that if friends were staying and, not being used to dealing with the media, would panic and immediately telephone him at Aldergrove. "Everyone being aroused at 5.30 am or 6.00 am is not really that amusing", he notes.

The Ulster Unionist leader is usually in his Westminster office which perches under Big Ben by 9.30 am. Mail is sorted and his secretary takes dictation. Between 10.30 am and 11.30 am there are usually appointments and meetings. The mid-day mail then appears and the process begins again. This time some of the correspondence may include aspects of policy which take longer to reply to. All is again cleared to the out tray.

The business of the House begins at 2.30 pm and on the three main full days when he is there – Tuesday, Wedneday and Thursday – he will attend from the beginning, particularly to listen to Prime Minister's Question Time or ministerial statements.

In between the office work and the day's business he will take a simple lunch in the cafeteria. Never one for pomp and circumstance or the Westminster members' restaurant where there is the traditional silver salver, Molyneaux prefers the self-service cafe. Scrambled eggs on toast would suffice most days of the week if they were on offer.

The main debate of the day usually begins at 4.30 pm and if it is noteworthy, he will remain in the green dominated chamber for its commencement. By 6.00 pm he is usually back in the office with more paperwork to do, the final mail sorted, and ready to be sent out. It could be anything from a letter from a student asking questions about a certain Bill or debate to a constituent who needs help and advice on how to tackle a benefit problem.

Vera, Molyneaux's secretary, has worked with him for 12 years. A calm, refined woman, she admits that he does have one characteristic which irritates her. It is his diligent and detailed replies to letters. Because he is a Parliamentary leader he is invited to functions across London. However he does not much care for this form of socialising and declines most. But a simple "thank you but no" does not suffice. He will go to great lengths to profer his apologies, explain why he cannot attend and will suggest that if they would care to write to him again at a future date he would do his best to attend.

They have never had a cross word and Vera describes him, in all his actions, as a gentleman. Anger, she notes, is only shown by the telephone receiver being replaced in a heavier manner than it should be. Another characteristic of the MP dealing with his secretary is that he will never inquire if she has done the requested work, rather it is phrased "Did I remind you to" passing the onus onto himself. This has not changed over the years. Then again it is part of the Molyneaux make-up.

Her only criticism is that he does take on too much work. He will simply say "It is no bother, I will do it" while she feels it should be left for someone else. This includes going to the library and photocopying Hansard for some sixth former with a project to do. To Vera this is insulting a party leader who should send back a reply of "Go to your local library and find out for yourself". To Jim Molyneaux it is part of the job.

Eight o'clock may pass and he will decide to revisit the cafeteria for a light supper. When he returns to the office, Vera will have left for the day. This is the period for quiet reflection and speech writing – a time he enjoys immensely. There may be a few private conversations but in the main this is the time when he revels in not being disturbed.

Towards the end of the main debate of the day he will pull on his jacket and take the lift down to the Chamber for the wind-up speeches. The main division will come at 10.00 pm but he may remain for the secondary business – perhaps a debate on an order or a motion finishing at around midnight. While such debates are seldom covered by the press, they sometimes do provide an opportunity to extract something of value to the people of Northern Ireland. The business of the day ends with the half hour adjournment debate which is the gift of Mr Speaker. For perhaps several weeks a back bencher will apply to raise a specific matter, usually relating to his own constituency, and in his 15 minute speech he will make a case which has to be responded to by the relevant Minister. Even though it is late Molyneaux will find out about the subject to see if it has any relevance or bearing on Northern Ireland.

If a Unionist member is speaking in the adjournment debate Molyneaux will remain. But even on an ordinary day he does not leave the precincts of Westminster until near midnight having carried out an average working day of 15 hours. It is why he rarely sees the inside of his flat.

A generally held view which is accepted like an eleventh command- ment is that the Northern Ireland MPs "loaf" around Westminster. Politics in Northern Ireland has become such a dirty word that to be a politician is tantamount to being mad. The community ignores the basic fact that the 16 men, with one absentee, who represent the Province within the Palace of Westminster reflect them. If they did not vote for them they would not be there.

People in Northern Ireland, maybe as a consequence of direct rule, have not used the Parliamentary system or their MPs as best they could. Molyneaux suggests that this is partially because of the "hangover" from the Stormont days. Unionists regarded it as their citadel – not Westminster – and therefore if they wanted a job done they went to a Stormont MP. London and the Northern Ireland MPs were looked upon as nonentities at an outpost. Several did not even live in the Province therefore the "hiding at Westsminster" opinion grew within the community over the years.

There is still that detachment from London – in spite of Molyneaux's own attempts to change the Unionist team into a small Opposition party. And Northern Ireland people, while tolerating 20 years of violence, are intolerant of their politicians and blame them for all their ills.

In June 1973, Molyneaux told the House of Commons that since the abolition of Stormont the previous year, an Ulster MP's workload had doubled. He noted then that the Secretary of State Willie Whitelaw had suggested that the former Stormont members could still deal with the problems of their constituents but this point was ignored.

Molyneaux's view was backed by "Union Jack" Maginnis who questioned other members by saying: "I challenge any hon. or Rt hon. member to find a group of 12 members who have had more work placed on their shoulders during the past 12 months than have the representatives from Northern Ireland". Little has changed, maybe because of the lack of powers at local government level, and Northern Ireland MPs, whether Unionist or Nationalist, still get the brickbats. Because of this lack of comprehension, confusion permeates through to Parliamentary procedure and how best to use it.

Molyneaux cites the lobby system as an exact example of how the Parliamentary workings are not used to their full. It could be anything from an aspect of farming to the clothing industry in Northern Ireland. When it would be beneficial to the concerned groupings to lobby the MPs a fortnight before the debate, to set out their arguments and enlist the respective politicians' support, they usually land at Westminster on the day of the debate and call the members out into the central lobby as the business continues inside.

This, the Unionist leader points out, may be excusable for a family firm man who is fighting a battle single-handedly but not for an organisation or union which should know better and pay staff as researchers.

"It is silly, for while you could be in the House, fully briefed and fighting a particular group's corner, there you are in the central lobby being faced with the arguments against the legislation for the first time. That is no way to mount an attack. But it happens over and over again no matter how hard you try to tell people at home how best to go about presenting their case."

Another characteristic of the Ulster public and its ignorant contempt for its politicians is the way MPs are asked to functions but will be urged not to speak in a political fashion.

"What are we but politicians? Of course after this length of time I am used to it and I do understand the uniqueness of our situation but no mainland MP would be treated in a similar manner. They are seen on occasions such as the opening of a school extension or a charity function, as representing the entire constituency and it should be the same here. It is a two way process, I know, but at times I feel the MPs are not given the credit they deserve for representing the broader constituency – whether it be with a Unionist or Nationalist minority."

In recent years Molyneaux, in the continuing broad church approach, has tried to encourage his senior colleagues to be spokesmen and specialists in certain subjects – from Ken Maginnis on security to Martin Smyth on health. According to the latter it has worked considerably well.

"Jim has never wanted to promote himself – he has never wanted to be a one man party. He sees no strength in that and that is where his philosophy about spokesmen comes into play. If a colleague had a particular gift then he used that in a specific field, instead of having leader's comments on everything à la Paisley. Jim, because of his broad church approach, allowed the Maginnis' to deal with security, the McCuskers' education, the Smyths' health."

However according to the South Belfast MP there is one drawback – in spite of the Parliamentary team's enjoyment of their own roles: "Within our own party we get criticism from people who say the Ulster Unionists never get press coverage. They are so used to seeing Paisley all the time whereas that is not Jim's approach. There might be an Ulster Unionist comment appearing each day in the press but because they are all different, people think the party is not being reported. But it is Jim's method, developing people in their own spheres and giving them their place.

"People in Northern Ireland do not realise how highly respected Jim is as a leader in Westminster. Because he is such a self-effacing person and partly because of the media's blindness towards him, his work and effort goes unnoticed in Ulster but not by the other leaders at the House of Commons. As a leader he is clear headed, he knows what his objective is and sticks to it."

Smyth as "an insider" admits that unfortunately, because of the independent streak, members feel they know best and at times go their own way. The old integrationist label resurfaces again.

"Jim Molyneaux from the very beginning was absolutely consistent. He believed there was a place for the close contact government we had in Northern Ireland, he used that phrase from Willie Whitelaw. However as an Ulster Unionist, he would not disagree if we were being governed like every other part of the United Kingdom. Having said that he recognises the necessity for responsibility to be put in the hands of Northern Ireland people so that they may look after their day to day affairs. Jim has sought to take us to the position where we have the highest degree of responsibility and power over our own lives."

Smyth who has known Molyneaux for many years through the Orange Order, also rejects the "Powell's poodle" theory. He points out that everyone in the Unionist team benefited from the former Cabinet Minister's intimate knowledge of Parliamentary procedure: "Jim recognises that he is not an expert in certain fields, Enoch is. But he has not been prepared to accept Enoch's word without evaluating it each and every time".

The South Belfast MP recalls a story which he believes highlights this aspect of the two men's relationship: "Enoch was always angry about people reading their speeches in the House. Now Jim is not entirely enthused at a deadwood reading but because Jim never had the experience of oratory in the way Enoch had, he always wrote down his notes to guide his thought process as he went on. Enoch used to criticise this until Jim said to him one day 'tell me Enoch which is the most heinous, to say what you want to say accurately and clearly in the House so that you can be understood by the people or to go up to Hansard afterwards and correct all your mistakes'".

Molyneaux still uses such subtle language and manoeuvrings in his dealings at Westminster. It applies, at present, to supply day debates. These are a vital part of the Opposition's armoury in attempting to embarrass the Government. They total about 20, a sizeable proportion of time out of each Parliamentary session, and the Opposition can use them to debate any topic. Usually it does its best to pick a date when its members know they can place the Government in an awkward position over a certain course it has taken. Such debates force the Government of the day to be answerable to Parliament.

Shortly after Molyneaux became the Unionist Coalition leader in the House, he was able to extract from the Labour Government a half supply day so that if there was an emergency in Northern Ireland, its members would have the right to bring it to the attention of the full House.

However he has been in an even stronger position – since the break-up of the Alliance between David Owen and David Steel. When the "twin" party was on its trail of success after the 1983 General Election, the two Davids were able to demand and succeeded in getting three of the Opposition's supply days as of right. They too, like Labour leader Neil Kinnock, used them to embarrass the Thatcher administration and promote their own cause.

But an off-shoot of the split and the relaunching of the Social and Liberal Democrats meant that the new Paddy Ashdown party fell foul of a Parliamentary Standing Order. It states that there should be 17 days at the disposal of the leader of the Opposition and three days at the disposal of the leader of the second largest Opposition party as elected at the previous General Election.

Because the SLD was not elected under this name but rather the Alliance in the 1987 General Election, they forfeited their three days which automatically went to Jim Molyneaux.

It is only three days each Parliamentary session so Molyneaux went to the Leader of the House John Wakeham and asked, so that it would be fairer to all minority parties, that they be divided into six half days. It was granted and it has meant since that the minority leaders must come to the Ulster Unionist chief to ask if he will allow them a half supply day to speak on an important matter whether it be tin mining in Cornwall or the latest outbreak of food poisoning. Because it is usually a Great Britain party and not either the DUP or the SDLP, the day is planned to coincide with a bye-election to ensure maximum publicity for the smaller party.

It is then up to Molyneaux to go to the Leader of the House and his civil servants and organise the date to suit all the members involved. The process may sound insignificant in the wider context of Parliamentary procedure and the administration of a Government, but it is another example of Molyneaux, in his quiet manner, continuing his promotion of the Unionist case at Westminster. The other leaders must come to him to ask if he will allocate them a half day and bargains have to be struck in the process. One day, maybe, the markers will be called in again.

There is also a subtle publicity exercise involved. When the day is granted it goes on the Order paper under the heading: "Supply Day; motion by the SLD. This is an Opposition half day at the disposal of the leader of the Ulster Unionist Party. The subject has been chosen by the SLD".

He has not availed himself of such a debate because he feels it must be of some Province wide importance rather than a constituency matter in Lagan Valley. He recognises that the mainland parties, no matter how small in numbers, want to gather mileage for opinion polls which do not have the same impact on voting patterns in Northern Ireland. To use such a debating luxury would have to be for a much more "high minded" topic.

"It could be opportune if, for instance, the Government gave an indication that they were going to increase the powers of local government. You could do something quite useful during such a debate. If you spoke to Labour and the SLD beforehand and ensured that they agreed with the wording of the motion then you could find you would have their support for something which called for an early start to be made on restoring responsibilities to elected representatives of local government in Northern Ireland.

If you got all Opposition parties to back this then the chances are that the Government would not vote against it. Then you would witness the pressure passing through Parliament onto the Northern Ireland Office who would then be questioned as to why a package was not forthcoming."

In this role, as usual, Molyneaux does not espouse it as an important aspect of his Parliamentary work. But it does highlight how he goes about his duties in an exact and proper fashion which is why others in the House hold him in such high regard. In Northern Ireland it goes unnoticed, partly because of his unwillingness to boast and partly because of the community's in-built disregard for what goes on at Westminster. It is all too slow and not instant enough for the Ulster mentality.

Martin Smyth believes Molyneaux's role in the allocation of supply days has earned him great respect from the other leaders in the House: "He does take a low profile but when he has to dig his heels in he does so immediately. An example of this was when the Liberal faction went and got itself a half supply day, while Jim had already granted it to the Owen grouping. He immediately went to the Leader of the House office and said this was wrong. They informed him that the week's business had already been arranged and he informed them that that was just too bad and that they had better unarrange it. Because Jim put his foot down the whole business of the week was radically changed and he kept his word.

"They have, on different occasions since then, tried to put him into a situation of compromise where they could pressurise him but he has absolutely refused to fall for it."

But Molyneaux's greatest achievement at Westminster has been the securing of an additional five seats for Northern Ireland. In 1973 he spoke in the House of the need for proper representation. As the member representing the then largest constituency in the United Kingdom he had had first hand knowledge of the difficulties it entailed.

The former Armagh MP Jack Maginnis, speaking in the Constitution Bill debate of June that year, noted; "If, in 1920, Northern Ireland had been granted full parity of representation with the most comparable area of GB – Glasgow and the county constituencies beyond to the north and west – we should have had 16 representatives which is what we are asking today". Later, in the same speech, he said: "Therefore, Northern Ireland should be entitled to full parity of representation with the rest of the United Kingdom".

This reflected Molyneaux's views entirely and he advocated them during the committee stage of that same Bill. However he was unable to act on them until the precariously balanced Callaghan Government of the late 1970's. Molyneaux found himself at the centre of negotiations to keep the Labour administration alive in March 1977, just a year after Callaghan had taken office. It was during this final period from that early spring to the end of the Labour Government in 1979 that Molyneaux's team was able to exercise its greatest influence at Westminster as a minority Opposition party.

Ironically devolution for Scotland and Wales was causing the administration to stare at the possibility of defeat. In February the legislative process to allow Scotland and Wales their own assemblies had ground to a halt and the fresh leader of the Opposition Margaret Thatcher tabled a motion of censure for debate on March 23.

But according to Callaghan, in his memoirs, both the Opposition and the press did not know how determined his Cabinet was to avoid defeat and so he began a process of trying to woo the smaller parties, including the Unionists, into supporting his administration.

Molyneaux recalls how that process began: "I was sitting at my desk on the Friday morning before the debate which had been set for the following Wednesday, speaking to Harry West on the telephone from Belfast. The call was interrupted by the over-ride which only Downing Street has the authority to use. A girl told me that it was indeed Downing Street and asked me to put down my receiver to wait for a priority call".

The party leader at the other end of the phone was bemused by it all and asked what was going on. Molyneaux replied, in his impish manner, that maybe the carpet in the office needed changing and the Prime Minister wanted to consult him on it. He told West he would ring back and waited for the call. It was a private secretary who immediately put the Leader of the House and the deputy Prime Minister Michael Foot on the line. The gentlemanly intellectual asked if the Unionist leader could come around to No. 10.

He quickly replied that he could not, he had a flight to Belfast booked with a string of engagements organised. It is a typical example of one of his characteristics – if he says he will be at a certain place at a certain time he will be, unless the elements have worked against him. On the other hand he is also intolerant of others who, by their personal make-up, are always late.

Molyneaux emphasised to Foot that it was not out of disrespect for the Prime Minister. He simply could not go but that he would be back on Monday. However it was arranged instead that he would be able to meet the Ulster Secretary Roy Mason and Foot at the latter's room in the House of Commons before he left for home.

They discussed what arrangements they could come to over the looming no confidence vote. Molyneaux bluntly said that nothing, at that time, could be done. All he could do, he said, was to set out the known Unionist position – equal representation in the House, a devolved administration in the Province and the restoration of powers to local government. Everything was discussed in general terms but he remembers that there was a little talk of the first item on his shopping list. He suggests that this was because Foot was already well-briefed on the issue by Powell, an admired friend.

The Unionist leader suggested that his troops could possibly co-operate if two of the three items on the list were granted but one had to be devolution – the mainstay of the Official Unionist Party's policy. Before the discussions ended he again stressed that his refusal to meet the Prime Minister was not a rebuff, left for Belfast and found the party officers backed his line.

Monday morning arrived and Jim Molyneaux was back in London and ready to carry out exploratory talks with the Prime Minister. He was called to the Prime Minister's room at the House of Commons and took Powell with him, Callaghan was accompanied by Foot. They had hardly sat down when the Prime Minister opened the discussions with a proposal which made the South Down MP tense up with surprise.

Callaghan made it clear that no matter how the talks ended or how the Unionists voted on the censure motion, he was going to ask the Speaker George Thomas to convene a Speaker's Conference to give Northern Ireland equal representation in Parliament.

The Unionist leader's reply was couched in the usual mixture of politeness and caution: "Yes, that is very, very helpful and we are grateful but for the purpose of Wednesday night it would have been of great help if we had crossed that bridge before now.

"The Prime Minister agreed and noted that if he had listened to Michael Foot ten months previously such a conference would have already been in existence."

On devolved government the talks were not as fruitful. The Unionist leader explained that through the Convention, set up by Wilson, his party was geared for devolution. However in quick reply Callaghan said it would be "too difficult" in the short term and he felt he could not deliver. On the third item, the restoration of some powers to local government, he suggested that talks could continue after the crucial vote.

However again Molyneaux emphasised that there had been three items on his list. He warned the Prime Minister that while he appreciated the gestures, there was not enough to see him through the vote. Callaghan retorted that they should reflect on what had been said and then they might meet again. But Molyneaux and Powell, in reality, could only offer a few votes so Callaghan turned to the Liberals under David Steel to secure the future of his Government. The Unionist leader had the difficult task that while his small band had severed its formal links with the Conservative Party they were still reluctant to give firm commitments to the Labour administration. He had to steer this difficult path throughout the next two years of the Callaghan Government.

The former Labour Prime Minister is slightly at variance with Molyneaux over that Monday morning meeting. In his memoirs he cites only two items – extra seats and devolution with no mention of extra powers for local government. But he does concur over the decision to set up a Speaker's conference and notes: "I later discovered that my unconditional readiness to refer the question of Northern Ireland seats to an all party conference, irrespective of how they voted on the no confidence motion had made a favourable impression and improved the atmosphere between us. Without being conscious of it, I had cast my bread upon the waters and later months were to prove the words of the preacher 'thou shalt find it after many days'."

Meanwhile Harold McCusker had, with his Parliamentary leader's approval entered into talks with Labour's Roy Hattersley – primarily over a natural gas pipeline to the Province. These proved fruitful enough for the Armagh MP to abstain in the vote. The "no confidence" motion was rejected by 322 to 298 – a majority of 24 – with the Liberals going through the Government lobby.

Callaghan opened the debate by outlining the various negotiations he had undertaken and began with the Ulster Unionists. Molyneaux takes up the story: "He informed the House, amid sneers from the Tory benches, that he had decided to ask the Speaker to convene a conference to give Northern Ireland equal representation. The Tories went wild at this, shouting accusations like traitor and bribe at me. I just sat smirking and Callaghan, in a way, was gently baiting them knowing that they were going to walk into a trap.

"At this point Michael Mates intervened and asked if the Prime Minister would categorically deny any deal was offered concerning the movement of two battalions of troops to Ulster as part of a political settlement. Callaghan, keeping his cool, said he could categorically deny that such bargaining ever took place and that there was at least one other person present in the House who could confirm it. There was a stunned silence and I stood up, as Callaghan had given way without my asking, and I said I was grateful to the Prime Minister for giving me such an opportunity to deny that any such point was ever raised. I said that we would both have viewed any such report with contempt. It was then the turn of the Labour boys to go wild and called on Mates to apologise and withdraw his remarks."

The rank and file Tories still believed that a deal had been struck between the Government and the Unionists. However in his traditional quiet manner Molyneaux, with Callaghan's knowledge, had already briefed Thatcher that there had been no agreement. Under the confidentiality rule she could not be allowed to advise her Shadow Cabinet, let alone the back benches on the state of affairs. Callaghan continued the speech outlining Molyneaux's shopping list but noted that the honourable gentleman from Antrim South had made no bargain with him and that he did not know what way he would vote.

Later in the debate there is a telling insight into Molyneaux's character as delivered by the present Trade and Industry Secretary Nicholas Ridley. He castigated the Liberal Party for entering into the pact with the Government by noting that for small concessions it had delivered its soul to vote with Labour.

However he continued: "I admire much more the hon member for Antrim South, the leader of the Ulster Unionists. He has gained much more. He has gained proper representation for Ulster, yet he will not vote with the Government and has no compact with them. That is the way in which to do business. The Rt hon member for Roxburgh, Selkirk and Peebles (David Steel) should take a lesson from the hon member for Antrim South on how to do a deal".

There was no contact for a couple of months after the March crisis. Molyneaux still wanted to press for improvements in local government but at the same time did not want to torment the Prime Minister with a barrage of requests – instead he channeled his concern through Roy Mason. Towards the end of 1977 he wrote to Callaghan, asking for a meeting to which Powell was also invited. The Unionist leader immediately noticed a change in the Prime Minister's mood – there was no conciliatory tone nor was he in a frame of mind to do business on Northern Ireland issues.

The two Unionists compared notes afterwards and concluded that Callaghan had been "mugged" by both the Foreign and Northern Ireland Offices. It was their punishment meted out to him for granting equal representation.

"This was the issue which they hated most. Both Departments loathed the very idea. Even though he was the Prime Minister Callaghan could not withstand the pressure once they had lined up all the forces and now we found that there was going to be absolutely no movement or improvements on the local government front", Molyneaux observed.

However while these negotiations were proving difficult, the Speaker's Conference was continuing. Molyneaux and Powell played out low key roles during its deliberations. They were confident enough about the outcome – the Government was committed to it and the Conservatives had been advocating it – the only decision the conference really had to make was on the number of seats.

Several leading party members at home demanded 21 seats but Molyneaux defends the 17 achieved: "We would have been asked for our advice, usually in private and not at the conference. Our view was that we wanted a settlement similar to the Welsh average which has a certain degree of remoteness. We did not want the same scale as Scotland for the simple reason that if some day Scotland gained devolution then its representation in the House would have been reduced. Scotland was, and still is, grossly over-represented, we did not want our settlement to be thrown into the same melting pot if we ever achieved devolution. We believed that if Wales received its own Assembly then it would keep its quota of seats, unlike Scotland so we used the Principality as our benchmark. The Speaker's Conference came up with 17 or 18 and after deliberations 17 was eventually the agreed figure".

A Bill then made its slow way through the Parliamentary procedure to ratify the increase while Molyneaux did his best to withstand pressure from the party at home to do all he could to bring down the Government. Members believed Margaret Thatcher would be a better friend to them. But his formula was that as long as progress was being made on the policies he wanted such as the extra seats then he would not seek to bring the life of that Parliament to a premature end. He had to keep repeating this over and over again in a bid to ensure that the Bill was written into the statute books.

As well as facing the groundswell at home for him to help bring down the Government, Molyneaux also realised that the Bill itself faced opposition from the Labour Left. They, like the West Belfast MP Gerry Fitt, felt it would benefit the Unionists and that they would gain the spoils of the extra seats. Its final night in the Commons came on January 17, 1979.

"Enoch and I thought about it and came to the conclusion that we had to use all the levers of influence we had to get the Bill through at all costs in the lifetime of that Parliament. Our opponents of course, the likes of Kevin McNamara and company, were equally aware of the situation. The crisis came at the Third Reading Stage when the Labour Chief Whip Michael Cocks came to me in the middle of the night and said he felt we were in trouble. He explained that he could not hold the pay roll vote."

The block numbers 120 members of government who have the task of sustaining the Government's presence and strength in the Commons at any given time. Molyneaux was also informed that the Chief Whip feared the back benchers were turning against the Bill and he could not contain the revolt. He took the information calmly and asked Cocks if he intended to hold them simply under his own authority. The Chief Whip replied yes but was promptly told by Molyneaux that there was a higher authority and where was the Prime Minister. Callaghan was in bed at Downing Street, Cocks was doubtful about disturbing him but Molyneaux insisted.

"Michael eventually agreed to telephone. He returned within ten minutes to tell me that he had roused the Prime Minister who had told him to issue an order to the troops. The message was clear 'I have promised Molyneaux he will get that Bill tonight and furthermore you will stay there, if necessary, until lunchtime tomorrow until you do'."

This was relayed to the Labour members, the rebellion fell flat on its face and the Bill went through its roughest stage within an hour on a vote of 104 ayes and 17 noes. It received its Royal Assent less than one week before the Labour Government collapsed in March 1979. Molyneaux had achieved one of his major aims as a Parliamentarian.

One of the negotiators intimate with the talks the Unionists had with Callaghan through those two final years of the Labour Government was Michael Foot.

He and Powell were already well known to each other and there was a mutual admiration but he had not known Molyneaux at all well. That has changed over the years. With his centre stage position as Leader of the House during those difficult times, Foot believes Molyneaux was a man of total integrity.

"In any of the discussions we had with Jim he never went back on his word or promised something which he then did not deliver. Of course we wanted to remain in power and used what skills we had to do so but Jim Molyneaux remained true to his principles throughout. I have nothing but admiration for him. We had frequent meetings, he and I, through those times and I can never remember Jim conceding any of his Unionist beliefs to gain glory for himself inside Westminster.

He pointed out that he had indeed been converted to the view that Northern Ireland should receive equal representation before the Callaghan talks of March 1977. The former Labour leader maintains the case for an increase of seats was overwhelming and something he felt the Government simply could not ignore – in spite of nationalist protests.

There was also opposition from inside the Cabinet from former Secretary of State Merlyn Rees. He had been against such an increase since 1972 and the imposition of direct rule. In his diary of that time he noted: "The Unionists have returned to the question of the 12 members at Westminster. We will have to be very firm. I am not interested in the case for six more members but I am interested in the case for Northern Ireland. The Catholics see the extra seats as a move to integration".

In his book on his time in Northern Ireland Rees admitted that while he was Secretary of State he could use his power to block the move but when it came to the Labour Cabinet in 1977 he was by then Home Secretary and the proposal was outside his "own patch". It meant his was the lone voice against Ulster Secretary Roy Mason, Foot and Callaghan in opposing the Speaker's conference on the issue.

However he has not changed his mind and recalls a point he put to the Prime Minister in the spring of 1977 when discussions were dominated by the Scottish and Welsh devolution plans.

"Northern Ireland's history and geography distinguishes it from other areas of the UK, as does the presence of two separate communities. Its problems are not those of Scotland or Wales and therefore do not necessarily require the same treatment."

In spite of this contrasting view on the extra seats Rees still believes that Molyneaux, with the help of Powell, steered the Unionists into becoming a more effective voice at Westminster and knowing the ways

of Whitehall. He describes Molyneaux as a "much underrated politician".

Foot too recognises this in the Unionist leader and also emphasises
that he understood the difficult path Molyneaux had to steer because of
the natural affiliation Unionists had with the Tory Party.

"Because of this it was difficult for Jim to carry on talks with us but he
did so with the utmost skill and never once went back on his word in any
commitment he may have made. I think he is an extremely capable
leader and one who most people in the House of Commons recognise as
such".

The heady days of the Lib–Lab pact, when minorities like the
Unionists took on an importance above their numbers, did lead to
exciting times at Westminster. The Unionists found that they did have
opportunities to influence government and Molyneaux used this channel when he felt it was necessary. But the one major concession was the
additional five Ulster seats and he never equalled it again in the
remaining months of that Parliament.

According to Patrick Cosgrave, again in his biography of Powell,
". . . the truth of the matter is that Callaghan's single concession to the
Unionists was of far greater importance than anything offered in the
way of cosy get togethers with the Liberals".

Throughout all the toing and froing Molyneaux kept his feet on the
ground and realised even then that the excitement would not last: "I
recognised that through those times, we were on a high but it was also
abnormal. I accepted that the situation could not or would not be
repeated. As Enoch said to me one day towards the end of that
Parliament that he could not expect the Almighty to be so good to us
twice in a lifetime. Of course there was going to be a low. Normality at
Westminster is watching a Government carrying out its legislative
programme with a workable majority. This was a peak period and one
which has obviously not been repeated since".

It was again a question of temperament. He had been in the
Commons since 1970 and while events in Northern Ireland kept hitting
the headlines work at Westminster, thanks to Heath's workable majority, went on at its normal pace. Having experienced that he knew the
period of drama and intrigue with the precarious Labour Government
would pass. That temperament was shaped during the war years –
particularly at its close. The excitement and urgency gone, there then
came the realisation that it was back to normality and, in many ways,
drudgery.

Powell recognised that Molyneaux was not an eloquent Parliamentary speaker but that this was made up by the fact that he was a real politician.

"He is somebody who knows what the House of Commons is about. What Government is about. One of Jim's great qualities is his patience. He understands that there are some things which can be secured only by time and which are not to be secured by argument or propaganda."

7.   Prime Ministers

In the eyes of Ulster Unionists Harold Wilson will never be forgiven for the utterance of a few words one Saturday evening in May 1974.

He was broadcasting a message to the people of the Province which was in the throes of the Ulster Workers' Council strike. The Prime Minister simply accused the loyalists of being "spongers on the British public".

They were enraged and even moderates who had not been invoved in the widespread action to bring down the power-sharing executive, joined the ranks to ensure an end to the Brian Faulkner headed body.

The entire unionist section of the executive resigned on May 28 – after Secretary of State Merlyn Rees said the Protestant backlash could not be put down by military action.

One local commentator Andrew Boyd noted: "Rees and Wilson, the British Army and the RUC all surrendered to the loyalists and allowed the power-sharing executive to collapse".

However Jim Molyneaux presents a different perspective on what were 15 tense and dramatic days in the life of Northern Ireland.

Molyneaux, through his quiet start in Parliament in 1970 as the member for Antrim South, has had the chance to look at and observe the work of four Prime Ministers in regard to Northern Ireland.

Each has varied in his, or as is the present case her, preoccupation with the most strife torn part of the kingdom but Molyneaux has always attempted to work with each, when called upon to do so, with an impartial and polite manner. Always polite.

The characteristics which always comes to the fore in such matters is that he always knows more than he is readily willing to admit.

Behind that polite and quiet exterior is a person who knows exactly what he wants, does his utmost to ensure it comes about and without the traditional Northern Irish politician's loud-mouthed approach.

Through his years in Parliament he has evolved a shrewd, highly refined political mind – at times too refined for the Ulster public which does not see the subtleties he is dealing with.

One tell-tale remark on his character came about in a discussion on Wilson's "reign" over Northern Ireland.

"You cannot really go around being a cheat – even if you want to. Being a wee bit subtle, bordering on deviousness is one thing – that, in a way, is the politician's trade. You would never achieve anything if as a politician you sounded off about whatever your objective was, because then you are letting the other side see your cards – whoever the other side happen to be at that given time. That is the problem. You must never let the other players see your cards. This is a fair enough attitude and it happens to be mine for better or worse."

It was from this background that he views the described weakness of Wilson and Rees in the face of the 1974 crisis as misplaced.

The South Antrim MP was addressing a meeting in Bristol University when the shock news came through in March 1976 that Harold Wilson had resigned. No one had suspected it, even though his health was ailing, and Molyneaux readily admits that when faced with reporters he asked: "What Prime Minister?" Unlike Wilson's successor Jim Callaghan, the Ulster Unionist leader had had no "tip off" of what was to happen.

A question was put to him about the fact that it appeared that the Prime Minister's relations with Ulster Unionists were not good.

This is something the Unionist leader never believed and in reply pointed out that many people had made a mistake as they had imagined that he, namely Wilson, believed what he had said about Ulster Unionists.

Molyneaux has contended that this misconception of Wilson applied during the drama of May 1974.

He believes the Labour Prime Minister was such a "subtle operator" that all the indications were that the "spongers" speech was calculated to have the affect it did have – namely the success of a strike which had seen the life of the Province come to a halt for 15 days.

The Unionist leader has argued that Wilson, underneath the calm Government face, did not believe in this "damned nonsense of a power-sharing executive and a council of Ireland", even though he was supposed to pay lip-service to it.

He maintains that the then Prime Minister's reason for not using the Army to crush the strike was based not on weakness but on democratic principles.

"I believe Harold said to himself, whether I like it or not, and I do not like it, the people of Northern Ireland have voted against Sunningdale and the power-sharing executive and, it is not impossible, that Harold said to himself, the sooner that debris is cleared out of the way the better.

Then the strike came. And, put it this way, he did not do anything to placate us. He did not say, and this might be the clue to it, he never said 'well, yes, this is legislation put on the statute book by the previous government. We see no reason why we should dismantle it. On the other hand, we cannot fail to take account of the results of the recent General Election which gave convincing evidence that the people of Northern Ireland, as a whole, are opposed to what has been imposed on them and Her Majesty's Government will take very careful note of that decision'."

Molyneaux has always emphatically believed that this is what Wilson could have said if he had wanted the executive to continue but instead he went for provocation and the "spongers" accusation.

He succinctly noted that with that one broad brush stroke on a Saturday evening, "all hell broke loose and the entire structure was swept away".

The Unionist leader also rejects the notion that Merlyn Rees was a weak and ill-informed Secretary of State.

Again Andrew Boyd said of the Welshman: "Rees was undoubtedly the most inept person ever to be given responsibility for the Six Counties. He seemed obsessed with the theory that the people of Northern Ireland themselves could find a solution to their internal problems".

The latter part of that view would be backed, in a curious way, by Molyneaux, who believes Rees may have given the impression of being weak.

Instead Molyneaux looks upon the Labour encumbent as someone who had his feet very much on the ground. Even at that time, he pointed out, Merlyn Rees was enough of a realist to go on resisting faulty advice given to him by the civil servants. That would have applied particularly during the whole period of the strike and its immediate aftermath.

He recalls a meeting he and the then leader of the Unionists at Westminster Captain Willie Orr, had with the Prime Minister and Merlyn Rees when it became apparent that the strike was to go ahead.

A Molyneaux "trademark" since he became an MP has been that Parliament is where the real business is done and if you are to have an influence you must attend.

At this time in 1974 Molyneaux frankly points out that he did not rank very highly in seniority within the party. However he and Willie

Orr thought alike and the leader and he discussed matters three or four times a day. This was why Molyneaux accompanied him to this vital meeting which was organised without publicity or fuss.

It proved lengthy and realistic. Both Wilson and Rees were well briefed on the mounting crisis and adopted a matter-of-fact approach throughout the discussions.

Molyneaux remembers a key statement made by the Secretary of State: "It was at this meeting that Rees said 'whatever else you may think of the Labour Party, we are not bloody fools. We know that the result of the General Election has rejected Sunningdale and the whole of the power-sharing executive. That is the verdict of a free people and Wilson, pipe in hand, nodded at that. That is why they did not suppress it.

Because he and Willie Orr were survivors of the Unionist old guard at Westminster following the February election, Molyneaux felt it was his duty to stay at Westminster in the hope of "doing some good" before the strike took hold.

That February election had seen the United Ulster Unionist Council return 11 out of 12 Northern Ireland members to Parliament. Their campaign was directed both against the principle of partnership with the SDLP and the idea of a Council of Ireland as envisaged in the Sunningdale agreement. It had adopted as its slogan: "Dublin is just a Sunningdale away" and by fielding a single candidate in each constituency achieved its widespread success. In South Antrim Molyneaux, in a 61.5 per cent poll, was returned with a 35,644 majority.

One of the requests the two Unionist politicians put to the Prime Minister during that crucial meeting was not to involve the Army and the UDR in any attempt to suppress the strike.

Wilson was non-committal about how the workers' strike was going to be contained as it was just in its early stages which was, according to Molyneaux, an obvious and natural attitude to adopt.

The Prime Minister asked how could the action be contained and the Unionist advice came back that if essential services were to be maintained then the RUC was the proper force to do it.

"We were not saying to him and Rees to use the RUC to break the strike. We were simply saying, if it is necessary to have some kind of intervention by the State to protect essential services like hospitals, then use the police. Please do not bring onto the streets the Army and the UDR. That was the main thrust of that meeting and I do believe it did have an affect on the Government and they did not do it. They never even attempted to do it", Molyneaux recalls.

The Ulster Unionist leader is convinced that Wilson respected the will of the people because "whatever else he was" he was a democrat and the "sponger" speech was not necessarily meant as an insult to the people of Northern Ireland.

"It was maybe a way of making them concentrate their thinking, deliberately allowing them to get their steam up and come to their senses. Maybe he was really trying to tell them, 'follow up the results of the General Election, clear all the debris away and see where we go from there'. That was why he then set up the Convention."

"That was why when I spoke to reporters on the day he resigned, I agreed that on the face of it relations were bad between Ulster Unionists and Wilson but that was in the mistaken belief that Wilson meant what he had said about Unionists."

However Molyneaux admits that not everyone in the Unionist camp at Westminster viewed the Prime Minister in such an impartial manner.

The first few months after the success of the workers' strike saw relations between the Labour leader and Unionists stretched to the limit. They believed that he detested them and would do all in his power to wrong foot them.

But again Molyneaux takes a different view after some guidance from a senior Labour figure and friend of Wilson. He warned the MP that he would be making a grave mistake if he took the Prime Minister at face value and believed that he hated Unionists.

"I was told that the reality was that Harold did not like or dislike anyone enough to act unless it was to some advantage. From then on I watched his tactics and your could see him playing one group off against another – even within his own party", he notes.

From March through to October of that year, Molyneaux believes he deliberately baited the Unionist members when he faced criticism from his own back benchers. The Prime Minister would find himself emersed in a serious row and Molyneaux maintains he would have caused a diversion using the Unionists as his prey.

"The way he did it was to throw away a line and he did it by insulting the Unionists. They would take it that way as he trailed his coat and they jumped on it. But it was all a put on so that he would get through Prime Minister's question time without too many attacks from his own side. I knew that but I suppose it was not easy for someone in our ranks who was comparatively new to the House, to realise it."

During this time Wilson was attempting to shore up a minority government, knowing that another election had to follow within a matter of months. Parliament was dissolved on September 20 – bringing an end to the shortest Parliament of the century. By then the Labour Government had been defeated 29 times in the two months before the summer recess.

The October poll proved little help to Labour, while the Wilson Government was returned it did so only by a narrow majority of three – 319 to 316. It was with this backcloth that Molyneaux now as Unionist chief in the House, decided it would be better for his ranks if an operation in fence-mending was mounted without any "sacrifice of principle".

He believes Wilson was not unreceptive to the approaches because of the slim majority the Prime Minister was holding on to. The Unionist leader admits that it was never all that friendly or close. However he does note that the two men recognised that, in a way, they were "birds of a feather". He explains it by pointing out that both of them could see around corners and identify what was coming up next.

From that basis the relationship did develop for the remainder of the Wilson stay at Number 10. Molyneaux cites an example during a heightened security crisis during the summer and the beginning of the autumn in 1975.

Even though there was supposed to be an open-ended Provisional IRA ceasefire, there had been an increase in the number of Protestants murdered. In September six men were killed during a raid on an Orange Hall at Tullyvallen in South Armagh.

The Prime Minister invited Molyneaux to fly to London during the recess to discuss the security situation. In spite of the mood in Northern Ireland, it was a relaxed meeting in Downing Street which was also attended by Merlyn Rees. During the course of discussions Wilson asked the Unionist leader "well, suppose you were Secretary of State what would you do?"

Molyneaux replied with long held views on the Ulster security situation. He spelt out clearly that he would select a "relatively small portion of territory", concentrate the intelligence services and the security forces on that area and "clean it up" by legally eradicating terrorism. The "package" he gave as an example was South Armagh.

He was pressed further on what he meant and he emphasised that MI5 should be used and the security forces should be spearheaded by the SAS. He went on to explain that if this "legal clean up" was carried out in one area of Northern Ireland then that hold could be consolidated and another area could be focused on. By carrying out such an operation he felt troops would not need to be deployed in areas where there was no need for them and all efforts concentrated on the "bad packages".

Wilson said he would think over the Molyneaux strategy. Nothing happened until the January of the following year when ten Protestant workers were shot dead after their bus was ambushed on the Whitecross/Newry Road.

During the night of that atrocity Molyneaux was called by the Secretary of State. He describes how Rees was in a worried state, something, he says, which did not surprise him as everyone believed the "balloon was about to go up". The Unionist leader deferred the invitation for talks at Stormont Castle until the next morning, explaining that Rees should try and get some rest and he would see him for breakfast.

Over the morning meal Molyneaux repeated his view that the Government should take on board the previous September's suggestion. But in quick reply Rees claimed that he had got it wrong and that they "did not need any more" SAS deployed in South Armagh. At this time the Government continually denied that there was such a deployment of troops in this area.

During the conversation Rees was summoned back to London for a meeting of ministers but before he left, Molyneaux again asked him to remind the Prime Minister about his package plan, whether he agreed with it or not.

At 4.30 pm that afternoon a communique was issued from Downing Street after the ministers meeting. It was phrased in the traditional manner – as a result of the worsening situation in Northern Ireland, the Prime Minister had made the decision to commit the spearhead battalion plus certain elements of the SAS to South Armagh.

When recalling this episode Jim Molyneaux did not sit back, grin and point out that it had been his September briefing which had convinced Wilson of the need for the SAS and concentrating security in one area. Instead he went on to tell of a meeting he had with Wilson in the division lobby a week later. The Prime Minister, smoking his pipe as usual, came up to Molyneaux, dug him in the ribs, and said "I suppose you might say with some justification it took me a long time to get around to adopting your suggestion".

Molyneaux replied: "No, I will not say anything of the kind Prime Minister. As long as you continue in well doing you and I will remain friends". It is this type of response which typifies Jim Molyneaux. This self-effacing modesty is not skin deep – he genuinely believes his role is to consolidate the best position for Northern Ireland as part of the United Kingdom, not his own political career.

The enjoyment of playing with words is also highlighted in a further more light-hearted encounter with Wilson. It was in the canteen at the House, Wilson had lifted a cold salad, while Molyneaux was waiting for a hot meal. He asked if he could by-pass him up to the pay-desk.

Molyneaux lifted his tray, stood back in mock military fashion, bowed, clicked his heels and said: "Prime Minister, I am delighted to yield to an expert in the art of by-passing".

Wilson laughed his head off – one shrewd operator to another.

Relations with Labour Prime Ministers have tended to be more convivial than with Conservative. The queue jumping incident highlighted that Wilson could take a joke and understood exactly what Molyneaux meant – there was a barb there. However the Unionist leader points out that if it had been a certain other Prime Minister he would have found himself in the Tower by morning.

It takes little investigation to venture that the man he refers to is Ted Heath whom he has described as the most arrogant Prime Minister ever. The widely held view that Northern Ireland is safer as part of the United Kingdom under a Conservative Government tends to dissolve on listening to Molyneaux describe his views of the occupants of Number 10 Downing Street. He angrily recalls that Heath abolished Stormont, not knowing what to replace it with while the present Conservative incumbent, Unionist that she might be, signed the Anglo-Irish Agreement.

In the interim, after Wilson resigned, under Callaghan's Government he secured the extra seats for Northern Ireland and praises the Labour politician for always delivering what he had promised – great or small. He notes: "Because there were a whole lot of simple things which happened, done on a man to man basis, and he kept faith on all of them".

The first time the two men recognised the existence of the other was when Molyneaux made his Maiden speech in February 1971. He had the distinction of being the first "maiden" to begin the debate on the Consolidated Fund Bill. During his opening remarks of a speech which was centred on the responsibilities and duty of a Home Secretary in Northern Ireland, Molyneaux made a direct reference to Callaghan as the man who had had the task in the previous government.

The South Antrim MP noted that no one could have failed to acknowledge that Callaghan had had a civilised approach to Ulster and that even those who had viewed the consequences of his policies with a degree of pessimism had never doubted his sincerity and his genuine desire to help. Callaghan suddenly went back to where he had been sitting and listened to every word of the speech. A few weeks later, the

Unionist leader was in the dining room when Callaghan asked if he could join him. During the course of the long chat, Molyneaux asked him if he could put a question to him. It was simply that if he had remained as Home Secretary and had not lost the 1970 election would he have abolished Stormont.

The reply came back "certainly not" and again Molyneaux asked why. Callaghan retorted that the reasons one would have had to have given for the abolition would have made it almost impossible to restore it and, he added, "with all our faults" the Labour party never creates a vacuum without having some idea as to how it is going to be filled.

Callaghan went on to explain that Unionists, like Molyneaux, probably blamed him for twisting the arm of the then Northern Ireland Prime Minister Terence O'Neill. He admitted that the Labour Government had openly manipulated the Stormont administration. The strategy, he said, was to keep the Stormont government in being and to persuade it that it had to come more into line with the thinking of Parliament. Molyneaux maintains that from the viewpoint a Westminster administration this was a logical policy.

The then Home Secretary had issued in 1969 what had become known as the Downing Street communiques which were regarded as reforms of Unionist Stormont and in them had reaffirmed "that responsibility for affairs in Northern Ireland was entirely a matter of domestic jurisdiction". He had also reiterated that Northern Ireland should not cease to be part of the United Kingdom without the consent of its people.

Molyneaux believes that Callaghan had a better understanding of the Province's affairs than any of the other front bench politicians but that this too was limited as being Home Secretary meant the Northern Ireland desk element in the Home Office was only a linkage and did not have a wide brief.

His next serious exchange came in 1976 when Callaghan took over from Wilson. There is no formal installation in such a "change over" of Prime Minister during the lifetime of a Parliament – the Opposition leaders simply say something polite at the first opportunity.

However Molyneaux was not expecting the reply he received when he stood up to deliver his few words. He expressed the hope that since the terror campaign against the people of Northern Ireland began when Callaghan was Home Secretary, so might it be brought to an end under his premiership. The new Prime Minister got up, beamed at him and said that he appreciated the words of the honourable gentleman, coming as they did from him and describing the member from Antrim

South as someone whose friendship he thought he could say he had enjoyed for many years. He added that he knew the services Molyneaux had done the people of Northern Ireland.

The tribute he paid to him also had dividends – in spite of other Unionist MP's questioning why he had done so. The entire Cabinet had been in the House to hear the Prime Minister's first speech and because of the glowing reply to Molyneaux he noticed a discernible change in their attitude towards him. It was as if they felt he knew the boss, so they had better keep in with him. From then on Cabinet members would seek him out and ask him his views on what was happening at a given time in Northern Ireland. It worked wonders, is how he puts it.

However the backbone of the relationship with Callaghan came during the first no confidence vote his Government faced from the Opposition led by Margaret Thatcher in March 1977.

According to Callaghan, in his memoirs, both the Opposition and the press did not know how determined his Cabinet was to avoid defeat and so he began a process of trying to woo the smaller parties, including the Unionists.

This aspect of the relationship is set out in another chapter in the book but throughout all the negotiations which ended in Northern Ireland gaining five extra seats, relationships between the two men were nothing but "cordial". Both have always got on well together and they trusted each other.

Throughout these talks and the subsequent unwritten support for the Labour administration, Callaghan and Molyneaux continually kept their word. Molyneaux believed that as long as progress was being maintained on policies which the Unionists could support then the group would not seek to "bring the life of the Parliament to a premature end".

He eventually saw the appropriate legislation for the extra seats through the report stage in the House of Commons in July 1978. Callaghan had again kept his word with the Unionist leader. So, according to Molyneaux, it would have been an act of "base ingratitude" if he had then decided to withdraw any tacit support he felt the Unionists could give the Government if called up to do so. It was put to the test almost immediately.

September saw another flurry of activity and rumour that Callaghan was going to go to the country. Colleagues believed the reports but Molyneaux had his doubts which were confirmed when the Prime Minister broadcast to the nation one evening. He said he felt it was his duty to continue the work his Government had set out to do, therefore he had decided to go on to complete his term and then the people could decide in a General Election who should govern.

The new session saw little being done with the Government being blocked over most legislation. Christmas 1978 came and went and the Powell family spent the holiday in Northern Ireland. As Molyneaux left his friend to the airport he asked him if he would transmit a message to the "top man". This was that Callaghan should not necessarily accept that he had altered his formula and that he was not convinced of the need to prematurely end the life of the Parliament – if some limited progress could be made on Northern Ireland.

On return to Westminister, Molyneaux received a friendly note from the Prime Minister, thanking him for the message and saying he had been encouraged by it. However the Unionist leader admits that Callaghan did absolutely nothing about it and there was no further communications between the two men.

The situation continued to stagnate until March when the Government failed to gain, in referenda, the 40 per cent of the total electorate needed to allow the Scottish and Welsh Devolution Acts to remain. Callaghan himself admitted that this was the death knell for his Government. Molyneaux again repeated his message to the Prime Minister and again another thank you note was returned but with no movement.

The Conservatives were hesitant about putting down another no confidence vote considering their defeat on the previous occasion. However the fate of the ailing Labour Government was decided when the Scottish Nationalists put down their own vote of censure.

Callaghan, in his memoirs, recalls that the Conservative Party gratefully latched onto it and the debate was set for March 28. The margin could not have been smaller – 311 votes to 310 with, ironically, Gerry Fitt abstaining – in spite of desperate efforts to dissuade him. He was still opposed to the increase in Northern Ireland seats, believing that they would benefit the Unionists. Eight Unionists voted with the Conservatives but Harold McCusker and John Carson remained loyal to the Labour administration.

Through the crisis Molyneaux was being wooed by the Opposition – primarily by the Conservative Chief Whip and later Ulster Secretary Humphrey Atkins. This resulted in Molyneaux voting against the Government. He felt he had a clear conscience as he had offered twice within three months to help – not to prop the administration up but to ensure that the lifespan of the Parliament would not be ended prematurely, so long as some progress was made on Northern Ireland.

He has sometimes wondered why Callaghan did not take up what he describes as that "life-line" and feels he got his answer weeks after the vote when he chatted to some of the Cabinet Ministers.

"Because they did not know what had gone on, they tended to blame me for the defeat of the Government – although they also blamed Gerry Fitt. They believed that Callaghan was just so weary of the endless battles, both inside the House and in the country with the unions, that he saw no point in going on."

Within 15 minutes of the Scottish Nationalists putting down their motion of censure Atkins rang Molyneaux to ask if he would come to his office to discuss the vote. He explained that Mrs Thatcher would also put down a notice of no confidence which would cap the Scottish Nationalist one, if the Unionist leader agreed to support her. He went as far as to suggest that they would be happy if Molyneaux added his signature to it.

With his usual caution he refused, said the only aspect he was prepared to consider was backing the motion but he needed a little time. This was not to consult with the other Unionist members, but to seek out Airey Neave, the Conservative Northern Ireland spokesman and Thatcher's right hand man. Molyneaux and Neave were sound friends, and the Unionist had been instrumental in shaping the section on Northern Ireland in the Conservative manifesto. This had been drawn up the previous September when the party feared there was to be a General Election called.

He needed to speak to Neave to be assured that certain policies would be pursued if the Conservatives won the pending election. He saw him in his office and said he wanted just one thing clarified – what was the scale and scope of the commission which would establish the framework for administrative devolution in the Province.

Neave replied with confidence that it would not be a Royal Commission which would have probably taken up to 18 months in its deliberations on how a regional assembly could be set up. Instead, he said, it would be a committee with a couple of experts who would be able to set out in detail just what legal changes would be needed and what sort of administrative control the new body would have.

He returned to Atkins, reassured by Neave – not about policy, he felt confident it would be implemented – but the time scale within which it would be carried out. He immediately told Atkins that he would deliver at least six Unionists, knowing that Harold McCusker and John Carson would vote for the Government.

However he recalls an excited Chief Whip in the division lobby on the night of the vote, using a few choice words, shouting at Molyneaux that he had dropped at least one and he was not going to win the motion. A confident Molyneaux told him to calm down – he would win by one vote.

"I knew and he did not, what was in the mind of Michael Cocks and Walter Harrison his deputy. They had already decided that it would have been wrong to bring a dying member into Westminster Hall, leave him until the vote was taken when someone went to certify that he was in the building." That member Alfred Broughton died in hospital a few days later. If the Labour Chief Whip had insisted that he was brought to Westminster the vote would have been tied and the Speaker George Thomas would have undoubtedly cast his vote for the Government.

Mrs Thatcher swept to power in May and installed her Chief Whip at Stormont, someone who quickly began to quiz Molyneaux about Northern Ireland and Conservative policy towards it.

Molyneaux recalls one of his first question and answer sessions with Atkins: "Humphrey said 'Jimmy, you and Airey were very close and you knew what was in his mind'. In reply I was able to enlighten him as to where we had all got to, particularly Mrs Thatcher, on the creation of a regional assembly and the transfer of powers back to the Province. These conversations continued until August when there is that traditional break".

But when Molyneaux resumed the conversations in September, there was a distinct coldness on the part of Atkins. He was still polite but he was not as forthcoming on policy and how it would be implemented. However he did commission the Stormont Environment Minister Philip Goodhart to explore the process of creating the regional council and, in addition, what extra powers could be given to the district councils.

Goodhart did carry out these discussions, indeed Molyneaux and others had a working dinner with him in a County Antrim hotel just weeks before Atkins announced plans for his round table conference on devolution. The Unionist leader showed his contempt for the operation in a House of Commons question when he reminded the Secretary of State that he had warned him of such high wire initiatives, emphasising that he would have nothing to do with it.

Behind this "highwire" act, Prior's rolling devolution scheme and Sunningdale, Molyneaux sees the hand of Lord Whitelaw.

"I am quite certain Willie Whitelaw was behind the round table conference. After all he too had been a Conservative Chief Whip, so had Humphrey, he had also been Secretary of State for Northern Ireland

and Humphrey was again following him. Naturally Atkins would have leaned on Whitelaw for advice who, I am sure, was not adverse to using bullying tactics".

He believes the noble lord has had a conscience about Ireland over the years and has felt that he had to try and undo some of the wrongs inflicted on her by England. As Molyneaux points out Willie Whitelaw was the only leading Conservative politician who was willing to sit down and talk to the IRA – although he publicly stated afterwards that it had been a mistake.

Molyneaux admits that when Stormont was abolished in March 1972 he, like so many other Unionists, blamed Ted Heath for its downfall. But he claims that the real culprit in 1972 and thereafter has been Willie Whitelaw. "This is a rather startling picture but it is nevertheless true", he notes. "Willie was basically an integrationist who regarded his 1973 power-sharing act plus Sunningdale as an unworkable nonsense from which, in his view, the logical and inevitable step was integration. He knew that the initiative which was to be foisted on us by the Foreign Office, the Northern Ireland Office and Irish opinion, whether from Dublin or America, would simply not work. But he allowed himself to be pushed along that road in the hope that he would eventually get his way. He would then have been able to say 'well,' that has failed, let us start to govern the place from here and ensure that fair play is done for everyone. That was what he was up to. But the trouble was that when he left Stormont, he was replaced by Francis Pym who was very weak and instead of him being able to face the fact that power-sharing would not work, something Willie could do, Pym allowed his staff to dictate.

"Willie was certainly not surprised when the Sunningdale house of cards collapsed. However it has meant that since he left, the Foreign Office and the Northern Ireland Office have been able to impose their will on every Secretary of State in order to prevent the setting up of a workable form of devolution or, for that matter, of integration. Instead they are content to keep us in limbo – we have not been given a stable form of government at Stormont nor have we seen stability through any form of workable government from Westminster."

After the collapse of the power sharing executive Molyneaux believes Whitelaw became "sour and embittered" because he thought everyone in Northern Ireland blamed him for the litany of disasters. The Unionist leader would assert that through this exasperation, particularly towards Unionists who had refused to be pushed into anything, Whitelaw decided to go along with any initiative put forward by a Conservative Secretary of State – hence Atkins' round table conference,

Prior's rolling devolution and most recently the Anglo-Irish Agreement. All, according to Molyneaux, out of a sense of frustration and bitterness that his own plan did not come to fruition. "It certainly is not out of any deep, political feeling. I have no doubt that back in 1973 when power-sharing was first muted Willie knew it would not work but he allowed it to go ahead hoping, in good time, that integration was the only logical step".

The Unionist leader believes Whitelaw allowed Ted Heath to go ahead with Sunningdale, knowing that once the Prime Minister was given advice from one quarter and convinced of it, he would not listen to any other arguments.

Molyneaux has little regard for the former Tory Prime Minister and has always maintained he was "unsound" on Northern Ireland. Heath gave him the impression of being cold and self-contained, a criticism he himself has faced. His first brush with him was in September 1971 when Parliament was recalled for an emergency debate on the worsening crisis in Ulster. Harold Wilson had put down a 12-point plan which included a minister in the Cabinet for Northern Ireland, an all-Ireland Council and proportional representation elections to Stormont. Molyneaux encountered Heath in the lobby and said to him "I do not think much of Wilson's contribution". The Prime Minister replied with a frosty stare and "Can't you ever be constructive". The relationship never improved.

Stormont was prorogued and Heath made a statement to the House that March of 1972.

On subsequent days as the Northern Ireland Temporary Provisions Bill was going through Molyneaux noticed that Heath, while appearing confident, tended to look anxious. The meaning of this observation did not become clear to him for over two years after Heath had lost the February 1974 General Election and the executive had collapsed.

Heath invited Willie Orr and Molyneaux to go and see him in the House shortly after the workers' strike had ended. He was very civilised and although not relaxed, was most concerned for their comfort asking them if they would like a drink. Something, Molyneaux points out, which had never been done before.

He said "well, it has all been a shambles hasn't it? What a great pity the Government had not stood firm. But the real disaster was those power station workers who got control of the switches". To Molyneaux, this was the key which unlocked the previous observation and showed the extent of misunderstanding he had of the Northern Ireland situation.

"Willie and I stared at one another, not believing our ears. He kept going back to his regret that the Government had not stood firm and that it should have brought in the Army. He never saw that the February election had indicated the extent to which the people of Northern Ireland had rejected the Sunningdale agreement – 11 out of 12 MPs saying no to it. Willie said that he had been in London holding the fort and it was maybe better if I explained what had happened. In his cold fish way Heath said 'oh, really, what have you got to say?' and I simply said that I wanted to convey to him the atmosphere which had existed in the Province during the strike.

I told him that I knew of 10 dairy farmers personally who, if they lived in England, would vote Liberal. However day after day they had poured their milk down the drains saying that if that was what it had to take to bring down Sunningdale then it had to be. Ted looked absolutely shattered. To my own surprise, he did not contradict me and claimed his reports had proved to the contrary."

However weeks later in a speech in the House, Heath said it would be incorrect to assume that the strike did not have widespread support. By that time Molyneaux's "illustration" penny had dropped.

His whole attitude, according to Molyneaux, was steeped in miscalculation. His view that the shutting of Stormont would bring an end to violence, whereas Molyneaux believed it gave the IRA an impetus to continue to fight for its goal, and the notion that the 1974 strike had only been supported by workers in key positions.

A contrasting view of Heath was expressed by Molyneaux's former party leader the late Brian Faulkner. In his memoirs, he describes Heath as "brusque and business-like" and at their first meeting in London in April 1971 said that the Prime Minister had reiterated that Northern Ireland would remain part of the United Kingdom so long as the majority of its people wanted to. The Northern Ireland Premier said Heath had assured him that his administration would not act like big brother and push Stormont around in public. He also believed that Heath was a "man of principle and strong character who would stand by us when the going was rough".

However he did agree on Molyneaux's observation that he was cold as he noted at a Chequers' meeting later that year that Heath was "more relaxed and expansive than I ever found him before or since".

He also, in an indirect way, confirmed Molyneaux's view that Heath had always hated an alternative argument when he had already taken advice. Faulkner recounted this when he flew to London in March 1972 to hear, for the first time, of the removal of security powers from

Stormont. At the Downing Street meeting, also for the first time in his experience, was Willie Whitelaw.

"After some time it was becoming clear that Heath had not been making an opening bid to soften us up, but had made up his mind before he met us and was presenting what amounted to an ultimatum."

This type of attitude which Molyneaux describes as "arrogance in the extreme" was also evident in the aftermath of the February 1974 election which was precipitated by the three day week and the miners' strike. Labour gained 301 to Heath's 297 seats. Northern Ireland had returned the 11 Unionists opposed to Sunningdale. The Conservative leader tried to hold on and began tentative discussions with the Liberals under Jeremy Thorpe.

Molyneaux who was his party's whip, telephoned Downing Street pointing out that there were at least seven Unionists who would automatically qualify for the Conservative whip. The Prime Minister ignored this information and eventually the Liberal talks collapsed.

The Unionist leader believes that, like Callaghan, Heath could have gained the Unionists' general support subject to consultation.

"That would have been the way another person with a bit of sense would have done it but he did not. I believe he, advised again by Willie Whitelaw, did nothing out of a fit of pique simply because we had been returned on an anti-Sunningdale basis."

He also observes that unlike the present incumbent at Number 10, he tended not to be able to brief himself properly and resented any advice. In contrast Mrs Thatcher has a peculiar habit.

Molyneaux points out that if the Government is faced with a serious problem, the Prime Minister will bring to the relevant Cabinet committee the expert in the department concerned and not necessarily the permanent secretary. This expert could be third or fourth in the civil service line and her approach is quite different from previous administrations when the advice was funnelled up through the stages in the department through the permanent secretary to the minister in charge.

Molyneaux will only sketch over the present occupant of Downing Street. His views on the Anglo-Irish Agreement and the Government's handling of the crisis are outlined in a much more detailed manner elsewhere. But he does believe she is a much more complex character than people give her credit for – not the school mistress image so many see.

In spite of the wide differences engendered by the events of November 1985, the relationship is beginning to come out of the deep freeze and Molyneaux is willing to suggest that there is a perceptible change in her attitude towards Northern Ireland.

However, throughout her time in Downing Street and before when she was Leader of the Opposition, she has sought him out for his opinion. Not that he would divulge the contents of such conversations to others. But it does help him in his long view.

8. People Power

In late April 1977 a motley group of loyalists, including several paramilitary figures and led by Andy Tyrie, called for a public strike the following month. The United Unionist Action Council wanted the weapon used to protest against security and a return of majority government to Northern Ireland.

It began on May 3, with little effect, many factories remained open and life went on as usual. The strike found few supporters among the wider loyalist community – in spite of it being backed by Ian Paisley and Ernest Baird, the former Vanguard chief.

The Official Unionists under Harry West refused to back the action, primarily because of the heavy involvement of paramilitaries. This decision had ramifications at Westminster as Paisley's decision to back the strike meant an end to the United Unionist coalition under Jim Molyneaux. Just four days into the stoppage its organisers were beginning to realise it was not going to work. The power workers, used so effectively in the 1974 workers strike, were wary of the entire operation and the men at Ballylumford refused to join its ranks.

On day six Paisley joined farmers blocking roads into his stronghold town of Ballymena but again there was little impact. On May 13 the stoppage was over, the DUP leader claimed it had been a success but his image was undoubtedly damaged – particularly as he had suggested that he would leave politics if it failed. The widespread view across Northern Ireland was that it had.

The relatively new Secretary of State Roy Mason was a completely different character to Merlyn Rees. He called a spade a spade and his background in the Ministry of Defence meant he was going to put security top of his Ulster priority list. He refused to be intimidated by the stoppage and counter-moved every effort made by the strike leaders to pull their stunt off.

There had been absolutely no discussion of such action within the Parliamentary coalition and its leader did not know exactly who was pulling the strings in its co-ordination in Belfast. The first Molyneaux heard of it was when it was announced on the news that it was to go ahead.

"The problem with the 1977 strike was that its declared object was to make Northern Ireland ungovernable until such times as Parliament restored devolved government to Northern Ireland. My simple view was that they could not possibly achieve that because a strike is in the nature of a bulldozer – it can demolish but it cannot construct. The same type of bulldozer was obviously very successful in 1974 because there was the structure in the Province in the form of the power sharing executive which had to prove to the world that it could run Northern Ireland. Once it was deprived of that proof and that authority by means of the 1974 strike, it had to go. Its authority had been completely lost.

"But in 1977 there was no structure to demolish. The Government of the United Kingdom was governing Northern Ireland by direct rule and could continue to do that regardless of whether the Province came to a standstill or not. The Northern Ireland Office could remain happy and secure at Whitehall and go on running Northern Ireland in a Parliamentary sense with absolutely no interruptions. It was only the administration which could be disrupted by the strike.

"Those behind the stoppage should have faced that problem before embarking on such an unwise course. The bulldozer had nothing to demolish. The irony was that the more successful they made the strike, the more unpopular it was going to be with the people of Northern Ireland.

"That was why the strike could not succeed in its objectives. It could succeed in making the Province a very uncomfortable place to live in for its inhabitants but it was not going to bring any hardship to Roy Mason and his ministerial team. They could operate from Whitehall and if anyone telephoned to complain to a certain department about services, the reply could come back 'It is not our fault, we are doing our best to govern Northern Ireland. It is your own people who are causing you this hardship'."

Molyneaux, like his party leader, realised the venture was doomed from the start. He had also quickly gauged Mason's character and knew that bullying tactics would not help matters with someone who was himself an abrupt character. In contrast Paisley and Mason did not get on from the start and jarred with one another on several occasions. It made the Secretary of State even more determined that the strike would not succeed. In June, however, he did announce that more troops were to be used in SAS type activity allowing Paisley to claim a hollow victory.

Molyneaux believes that those involved in the direction of the abortive strike had not thought the process through. They simply thought there was going to be a re-run of the 1974 operation, not realising that the scene and stage props were totally different, he also applies this to some of the younger Unionist politicians who were involved in the co-ordination of the Day of Action in March 1986 in protest at the Anglo-Irish Agreement.

"They felt the talks we were having with the Prime Minister were too slow. They would take too long to complete and nothing would come out of them anyway. They wanted instant action, an instant decision, an instant end to the Agreement. To me it was completely unreal to think that that would happen."

An accusation which has been levelled at Molyneaux through the years, like other leading Unionist politicians particularly Paisley, is that they "court" favour with the paramilitaries when it suits them. In actual fact Molyneaux has never had and has never wanted to have any dealings with an aspect of Northern Ireland life which has become part of the landscape. His suspicion and mistrust of such partisans who are ultimately not accountable to anyone but themselves is rooted in his wartime experiences. His caution began during the Second World War when as an aircraftsman at Dyce, Aberdeen, he began to realise that nothing was as it seemed on the surface. He watched two Spitfires escort the very latest Junkers 88 nightfighter into the station. The immediate reaction from the men was one of "what are those bastards doing here" but then Molyneaux began to ask questions to himself. Why had this German plane flown all the way from its base without being shot at? Why had the two planes known where to meet it and why had the defence arms at the aerodrome been told to "stand down" to allow the enemy plane to land? He found out that British Intelligence had influenced a Luftwaffe pilot and his co-pilot to defect with the very latest information on the aeroplane he was flying. The "devious" mind continued to question situations when he was transferred to Tangmere. There, an area of the aerodrome was sealed off and ordinary servicemen like himself were ordered to stay away. Again he found out that behind the screens sat Lysanders "dragonfly-like" aircraft with the capability of being able to land and take off quickly in nothing more than a large field. After piecing it all together, Molyneaux learnt that his base was being used as the only forward station to land and bring back British agents from occupied France.

He thought it all very brave and admirable until he too found himself in France after the Normandy landings. Because of his own small insights, he was able to sketch an overall picture on how operations were devised and then carried out but he also witnessed the seamier side of what was going on. He found out that not everyone involved in the Resistance were the noble, brave people he thought they were from his safe base in England.

His first contact with the movement came after the initial push away from the Normandy beaches. His unit's job was to secure an airfield on the left of the main column of the British Second Army, to give it air cover and organise the movement of supplies up to the front. Because of the nature of its job, the unit needed information about which fields were mined or which bridges sabotaged. This was were they found the local Resistance invaluable as guides. But while so many were indeed brave and honourable, a different aspect became apparent as the unit attended different villages' liberation parties as the Allies advanced. Molyneaux and his colleagues heard of individuals betraying others in the movement to the Gestapo, for no other reason than that they had a grudge against them. The ramifications of such actions were horrific. People were tortured until they gave up all the information they had so that an entire network was wiped out.

The young aircraftsman witnessed jealousies between local commanders which were so great that they probably hated each other more than the Germans. As soon as one had the opportunity to denounce the other as a collaborator, the innocent party was shot by the Resistance with no evidence against him and no trial. Animosities grew as petrol and food supplies began to flow in. The black market was rife, aided and abetted by servicemen, but when members of a local Resistance network were invited for a drink by the unit they would deny that they were involved or that there were inter-movement murders.

"They would say to us, we are fighting the Germans, we are not fighting each other and yet we had possession of the dead bodies and knew they had not been shot by the enemy."

The instability of such an organisation was brought home to him when he was involved in a rescue operation of an RAF radar unit on the Cherbourg peninsula. The small convoy stopped in a typical Norman village square and had drinks and a conversation with the local people. Shortly after they moved on to continue their mission, the village was shelled by a retreating German artillery unit.

The convoy returned the next day, after successfully completing their operation, to find five bodies hanging from trees and lamp posts in the same square where they had sat 24 hours earlier. They asked what had happened and were promptly told that the dead had been the villagers who had betrayed them to the Germans. The shells had been intended for the convoy – not the village.

"Without any proof, some had assumed that these people were indeed traitors and had carried out what was nothing more than summary executions without a shred of evidence. It was very easy to have a whispering campaign with absolutely no proof of any crimes. After several months you began to be disillusioned, not with the thousands of excellent people, but the vulnerability of such an organisation to be exploited by one or two bad apples. It made me suspicious and guarded of any such movement ever since. It is why I have never advised anyone to join the paramilitaries in Northern Ireland."

But this assertion leads to a contradiction because in 1972 he understood why men from the Unionist community joined the vigilantes – the loose grouping which became the UDA. The "B" Specials had been disbanded, the RUC disarmed and many in the majority community felt they were being left prey to the IRA. On July 1, 1972 the UDA set up their own no-go areas in Belfast and copy-cat acts took place across Ulster.

A few miles away in Lisburn, Molyneaux found himself nodding "hello" to masked men as they lined part of the route of the traditional Commemoration of the Somme parade through the staunchly loyalist town. The security forces, particularly the British Army, had advised the organisers that they feared a Republican attack and warned them that they could not give them a proper degree of protection. A unit of the newly formed UDA in Dunmurry, masked but unarmed, said it would line what they felt was the must vulnerable section of the route. They marched up each side of Wallace Avenue in the town and stood as the parade went past.

Molyneaux and others at the head of the procession were in the ludicrous position of nodding "hello" to these men: "You had the feeling that they knew you and vice versa on Christian name terms. If they had taken off the masks most of the officers and I would have recognised them. It was that type of contradictory position. They felt they had to band together to protect their own community.

"However, even then at the back of my mind, I was wondering will somebody be able to keep control of all of this so that we do not witness the same corruption and in-fighting as I had seen in the Resistance movement in Europe. Sadly, by the mid and late Seventies my worst fears were confirmed. The organisation had been penetrated and racketeering and intimidation had become hallmarks."

Loyalist paramilitaries' first major centre stage role in life throughout Northern Ireland came during the successful Ulster Workers' Council strike of May 1974 which saw the downfall of the power-sharing executive. Then they sat side by side on its co-ordinating committee with the political leaders, Paisley, West and Craig. This "power-sharing" of a different kind is a stigma the Unionist political leadership has failed to shake off ever since.

However Molyneaux, in comparing the two loyalist strikes, points out that those 15 days in May succeeded because the majority of Unionists were totally opposed to the Sunningdale agreement – the power-sharing executive and its Council of Ireland. He remembers the night after the agreement was reached in the Berkshire Civil Service College on December 9, 1973. His telephone did not stop ringing with messages of outrage and anger at what had been agreed. He took up the tale with the Secretary of State Francis Pym in the members' tea room at Westminster a few days later.

The South Antrim MP congratulated the Stormont incumbent who was nicknamed the "unknown" Secretary of State, as someone who was going to go down in history as an achiever. Understandably, the Cabinet Minister did not recognise this as Molyneaux sarcasm and thanked the MP for his praise. He did not know what was going to come next.

"Whether you know it or not Francis, in your very short term in Northern Ireland you have achieved what no other politician, unionist or nationalist, has ever been able to achieve – you have brought together in one force the self-styled working class and the professional class. They are as one now. They are utterly opposed to Government policy."

The Secretary of State pointed out that such a statement was Molyneaux's own opinion but the MP quickly replied that it was fact and repeated to Pym the deluge of calls he had received the previous night.

"They were not from hard-liners in Lisburn or Rathcoole. They were from middle class and upper middle class people who made themselves known. They told me in cultured tones that what had happened had been so dreadful that I could be assured of their support, no matter what course of action I took. These were people who I know in the past would never have thought of voting for me. They were completely adamant that they would have absolutely nothing to do with the agreement or its implementation."

The Secretary of State looked shaken and asked what was going to happen. He was confidently told that the executive would not function and the entire policy would not last. Within a month of that prediction the Ulster Unionist Council had rejected the Council of Ireland. Three days later Brian Faulkner, appointed chief executive of the power-sharing administration, had resigned as party leader, leaving it in disarray but opposition to Sunningdale intact.

The depth of such opposition was gauged in the February General Election – the now united unionist opposition to the agreement gained 11 out of the 12 Westminster seats but Faulkner clung on. Rumbles of strike action continued to gain momentum – rumour was rife at a conference organised by the United Ulster Unionist Coalition in Portrush that April which called for a complete renegotiation of the constitutional settlement. However few politicians wanted to move away from the parliamentary procedure, in spite of continuing angry scenes at the Stormont Assembly set up under the previous year's Constitution Act.

It was this Assembly which found itself the focus of attention when May 14 was circled as the day on which the strike would begin. The Stormont body, after several weeks' debate, was to vote on the Sunningdale agreement. The debate had spanned such a time scale because it was really a private member's motion put down by John Laird who had taken over the reins of administration at Glengall Street under the new leadership of Harry West. The debate on the Constitutional Settlement (Re-negotiation) 1974 had begun on March 19. It was punctuated with heated exchanges and personal abuse as Opposition members maintained the General Election of February 28 had shown the Northern Ireland people's rejection of the agreement and that the constitutional settlement should be renegotiated.

The chief executive moved an amendment to it backing the agreement as it stood but he was interrupted more than 150 times as he did so. That morning the News Letter carried an advertisement warning members of the executive that a full stoppage of industry would follow if the motion to implement Sunningdale was passed.

Ulster Workers' Council leaders sat in the public gallery as the vote was taken at 6.00 pm. There were three defections from the Government side to the anti-Sunningdale Unionists but the executive still won through by 44 votes to 28.

There was an immediate threat of power cuts announced to the Northern Ireland public by Harry Murray – a voice to become well-known across the Province over the next 14 days. He did so from the BBC's television studio in Stormont, shortly after the Assembly vote result was known.

At first there was little reaction – even less at Westminster where the Unionist MPs were informed by the news media. Ian Paisley went to Canada to bury an aunt. The following day power cuts forced factories to close and Belfast's Harland and Wolff shipyard went on strike. John Laird, whose motion had failed but had proved the deadline for the strike, recalls the strength of feeling in the community. As someone who backed the downfall of the executive, he was slightly wary of doing his family's traditional Friday evening shopping soon after the strike began.

He queued, like everyone else, outside a shop in a suburb of Belfast but to his amazement, rather than being shouted at and accused of bringing hardship on everyone, people came up to him, shaking his hand and slapping him on the back.

"It was incredible as I did think I would face a torrent of abuse. Instead I was getting comments like 'We are behind you Mr Laird, keep up the good work'. There was that type of reaction from everyone I met. There was this spontaneous feeling that what was going on at Stormont was wrong and it had to be brought to an end."

But there was widespread intimidation during the first few days of the strike to ensure that it would be a success and the paramilitaries gained the upper hand on the co-ordinating committee chaired by Derry Vanguard leader Glen Barr. Meanwhile Molyneaux spent most of the time at Westminster defending the action to other back benchers who did not understand the depth and strength of support the strike was receiving from people throughout Northern Ireland. He did attend several rallies during the period, particularly in the Newtownabbey area of his constituency but he never was at the centre of events – the political side of the strike was left to the Big Three. He does, however, vividly remember, like John Laird, how solidly people were behind the stoppage from the dairy farmers pouring milk down the drains to upper middle class people coming up to him and ensuring him of their vote.

Back at Stormont the Secretary of State Merlyn Rees was under seige, billeted with his ministers watching power supplies dwindle. There was a rota system for lighting homes, extensive limitations on petrol and rationed food supplies. The entire strike operation was being co-ordinated from the Gothic headquarters of Bill Craig's Vanguard Party in Hawthornden Road in east Belfast. Farmers' representatives and the CBI religiously made their way there to ensure they received their quotas of "safe passage" passes. As Merlyn Rees noted in his reflections of his time in Northern Ireland: "The way people distanced themselves from the British through the stoppage was remarkable".

The paramilitaries were enjoying their newly found responsibility too. John Laird recalls the scene outside the strike headquarters one sunny May afternoon: "There had been a meeting of the co-ordinating committee and Harry West had come out on to the street to find his car had a flat tyre. Two or three of the lads were standing at the door. Did they help? No, Harry had to take off his jacket, roll his sleeves up and get on with it himself. To me that epitomised the change that had taken place. They were sure of themselves, they had no need to help the leader of the Official Unionist Party".

Rees admitted that the Government was beaten "technically on all aspects of the strike and the Army could not guarantee to protect power stations or the pylons". On one day a total of 2,000 men – 1,500 troops plus RUC was needed to keep the five main roads into Belfast open. The strike organisers began to scent victory on May 22. While the executive continued to refuse to negotiate with the UWC it decided to rephase Sunningdale and the Council of Ireland. The first phase, a council of Ministers from Northern Ireland and the Republic would act in complete harmony on economic and social matters. A second phase which would give the Council greater powers, would only be implemented after Assembly elections in 1977/78. At first the SDLP rejected such a change but after a plea by Rees' deputy Stan Orme the vote was reversed. A meeting at Chequers the next day between the PM and the leading figures in the Stormont body – Brian Faulkner, Gerry Fitt and John Hume – resulted in a statement being issued which reiterated that there would be no negotiations with the UWC and that power-sharing was the only basis for the peace, order and good government of Northern Ireland.

Meanwhile with the UWC taking over petrol stations the Minister of Commerce John Hume had a plan of action for oil supplies which was due to be implemented during the night of Sunday May 26. The Army was to take over selected petrol stations which were then to be manned by civil servants. But 24 hours earlier the Prime Minister made his infamous "spongers" speech and threw thousands more loyalists behind the strike. Everyone knew it would only be days before the executive collapsed. The UWC issued a new threat – it would pull the plug on all electricity supplies if the Army continued to provide guards at petrol stations. Glen Barr announced that Ballylumford would close and electricity, gas, milk, bread and animal feed would also become the responsibility of the Army.

On the morning of May 28 the chief executive met his backbenchers, knowing support for him was diminishing. He was told, in no uncertain terms, that if he did not talk to the strike organisers he would lose their backing. Faulkner resigned, refusing to give in to such demands and at 2.00 pm Merlyn Rees issued a statement pointing out that he had accepted the chief executive's resignation and that under the terms of the Constitution Act 1973 there was now no statutory basis for the Northern Ireland executive. He stressed that arrangements existed for the continuing governing of Northern Ireland in accordance with the act. In particular, he said, the Secretary of State remained responsible for the preservation of law and order.

Within 24 hours the UWC had announced that the strike was over but still insisted that fresh Assembly elections should be held. Rees himself admitted that the UWC had had a great victory: "They had succeeded because of their control over electricity supplies and the massive support from the community". And in a private minute to the Prime Minister he also noted: "I feel strongly that there was, and is, no way of putting down an industrial/political dispute supported by a majority of the community".

However this point was lost on most members of the House of Commons. Molyneaux, a junior in the ranks, had attempted to get the message across that the vast majority of law-abiding citizens in Northern Ireland had supported the strike, if not the intimidation. He and Willie Orr attempted to tell Ted Heath, now leader of the Opposition, how strong such support had been – in spite of his insistence that if the power workers had not backed the stoppage it would have failed.

But the penny had dropped by the time the Commons debated the strike and its consequences on June 4, 1974. Then Heath noted that the continuing delay by the Government in taking action against the strike leaders allowed them to appear as victors: "It was at the point when the strike appeared to be a success and when the Government did nothing about it that support was mustered and there is no doubt about the breadth of that support".

Later in the same speech Heath highlighted the suffering both communities had gone through since 1969: "Catholics and Protestants have suffered from the activities of the IRA, Protestants have suffered from changes in institutions which had become familiar to them, deeply embedded in the political life. For five long years they have endured an almost intolerable condition of life in the Province of Northern Ireland. I believe that that lies at the root of the protest".

Almost 12 years later they were back on the streets again – this time in what was known as the Day of Action against the Anglo-Irish Agreement, March 3, 1986. Again there was intimidation and violence. The 24 hour stoppage, backed by the Unionist joint working party but reluctantly by the two leaders, was a graphical show of the wider majority community's opposition to the accord signed at Hillsborough less than five months previously by the London and Dublin governments.

It was almost like a blood letting – several younger Unionist politicians wanted to hit the Government hard and the only way, they felt, they could do this was by organising such a strike. They wanted a re-run of the 1974 action with the same outcome, the immediate removal of an agreement. But like the abortive 1977 stoppage, they failed to recognise the different circumstances.

During the day there was rioting and looting in east Belfast, a 300 strong mob petrol bombed the police on the city's Upper Crumlin Road and cars were set alight at Donegall Pass. In Lurgan two police families were driven out of their homes while the RUC was stoned in nearby Portadown. Hundreds went on the rampage during a "Death of Democracy" rally in Belfast city centre with shop windows being broken and a car showroom vandalised.

The police said there had been numerous reports of lawlessness across the country and RUC chiefs maintained the violence had been worse than anticipated. The Chief Constable Sir John Hermon said it was anything but a day of lawful protest, while the Belfast Chamber of Trade labelled it "disaster day".

Molyneaux had never approved of it and critics of the Unionist leadership quite rightly questioned the control Paisley and he had had over the whole affair. On the night of March 3 he issued a statement condemning the violence and admitting that it would do "terrific damage" to the loyalist cause.

But such action which had meant the closure of most industries, massive power cuts and a halt to air travel, had been rumoured even before the two leaders had their fateful talks with the Prime Minister at Downing Street on February 25. The *News Letter* of that morning noted: "both men know it would be pointless to threaten the once labelled Iron Lady with a loyalist strike" but the report went on to say that a one day stoppage was "very much on the cards" and could take place before the mooted date of March 3.

Molyneaux went to London not realising how far down the road to such action the joint working party had committed itself. The previous day he had cautioned people against expecting anything too spectacular from the talks. The two men were going to London to simply ask the Prime Minister if she was prepared to put the agreement on ice so that round table talks on devolution in the Province could get underway. The Ulster Unionist leader also warned that if they were given the "brush off" by Mrs Thatcher they would be seen as "extinct volcanoes". This, he said, could open up the door to non-elected elements and actions being taken which he and Paisley would disapprove of and, he emphasised, he did not know about plans for a loyalist stoppage if the London talks failed to get anywhere.

"If a stoppage became necessary I could only support it if it was designed to put pressure on the Northern Ireland Office and cause no hardship to the ordinary people of the Province." Neither he or Mr Paisley, he said, was involved in organising any strike.

The two men flew to London realising that they were to face a hard session with the Prime Minister and Ulster Secretary Tom King by her side. She repeated time and time again that the Agreement was designed to bring peace, stability and reconciliation to Northern Ireland and they repeated time and time again that the London/Dublin accord would not achieve such laudable aims. The next day when Molyneaux reported to the Stormont Assembly on the talks he told members that on at least 17 occasions during the meeting Mrs Thatcher stressed that she was committed to implementing the agreement. "It was a rather irrelevant answer to some of the points that we were putting forward, and it led me to believe that in her heart of hearts she could not find a viable and convincing answer to those points."

But there were the lighter moments too during the stern hour and a half long meeting. At one stage the DUP leader raised his voice slightly to inform the Prime Minister that Unionists would never stand for the agreement. In her best holier than thou voice, the Prime Minister replied "Mr Paisley, I ask you to believe I am a Unionist just as you are, I too am a Unionist". Paisley had been writing something down as she made this assertion and looking over his glasses replied "You have a very odd way of showing it".

Molyneaux felt the Prime Minister was doing her best to keep the talks going – not just for public consumption but that she herself wanted them to continue. He knew that the meeting was in deadlock and no further progress was to be made that day.

"I always instinctively feel that if you allow a meeting to run too long that you sometimes do damage. So I asked her if she was, at least, prepared to think about what we had said. This was answered in the affirmative. Then I pointed out that we would think about what she had said but that I was pessimistic unless her Government recognised that the situation in Northern Ireland was impossible for the pro-Union people under the agreement. We had referred her back to the two meetings we had had with her in the run-up to the accord and emphasised that we were not facing her with negative policies. We suggested that if she had agreed to take our proposals on board at the time, including a conference on devolution, then her Government would not have found itself in such a position. She agreed to reflect on these proposals as well."

They hoped to meet again within three weeks and both sides regarded the meeting as adjourned. A civil servant had scribbled a press statement which was perused by the two Unionist leaders, changes made and then approved. It was five simple paragraphs, one of which re-affirmed the Prime Minister's commitment to the Anglo-Irish Agreement.

But the fourth paragraph was the most significant. It stated: "It was agreed that the Prime Minister and the Unionist leaders would reflect on the various suggestions that had been made and would meet against shortly. It was understood that, if after discussion with all concerned the ideas raised in our talk today bore fruit, we should need to consider what that meant for the work of the intergovernmental conference." Molyneaux told the Assembly the following day that the only agreement they had made in the statement issued by the Downing Street press office was "It was agreed that the Prime Minister and the Unionist leaders would reflect on the various suggestions that had been made and would meet again shortly".

After the Downing Street meeting the day grew steadily darker for the two leaders. They had booked a room at Westminster Hall to meet the gentlemen of the press and there the confusion began. They recounted the meeting and emphasised that both sides had agreed to reflect on positions and policies. In answer to a question on political movement, Molyneaux replied: "We are not at the end of the road. The door is not slammed. We have got away from what was anticipated to be a deadlock situation".

The confusion was added to by the Secretary of State who appeared on the steps of Downing Street in buoyant mood. Mr King informed the press that "suddenly there was an opportunity to look afresh at a range of any possibilities. I hope people will enter that in a common constructive spirit" and warned against a loyalist strike. Meanwhile in Belfast members of the joint working party viewed the outcome of the talks as capitulation, the wheels were already in motion for a strike and the two leaders had wrung absolutely no concessions from the Prime Minister.

A few hours after the meeting Mrs Thatcher informed the House of Commons that she had had a "very useful meeting" with the two leaders and she saw "no possible reason" for the suggested all out strike the following Monday. Back in Belfast there were other views. DUP chief whip Jim Allister said the Prime Minister's response had been a "dictatorial" rejection of the ballot box and Unionists would not allow themselves to be deflected from a "smash the agreement course". Party Assembly member Ivan Foster called for "all out war" while party colleague Mid Ulster MP the Rev William McCrea said "muscle had to be shown".

The singing politician had sat with his party's deputy leader Peter Robinson at the back of the room where the two leaders held their press conference. One report suggested that when a reporter commented that everything appeared to be satisfactory Robinson muttered "wait until we get them home".

Unknown to the two chiefs the media, particularly in Northern Ireland, had seized on the phrase "deadlock" and that it had been broken. This led to a misplaced belief amongst the wider community that a breakthrough had been achieved. Meanwhile the party troops were seething. They could see no evidence of such a breakthrough and wondered what the two men were playing at. Paisley arrived back in Belfast before Molyneaux who held a Parliamentary party meeting after the press conference to tell his colleagues what had happened. Two of them, party whip Willie Ross and Upper Bann MP Harold McCusker, also attended the joint working party meeting to be held that evening at 8.00 pm in Ulster Unionist headquarters.

Molyneaux dutifully arrived in Glengall Street to be faced with a frosty air. Two of the working party, general secretary Frank Millar and barrister Peter Smith, were already in the office and conversation became formal and cold as soon as the leader walked in. The meeting was even worse. The two men reported that Molyneaux's advice was that in light of the Prime Minister's undertaking to consider and reflect upon what had been said, it would be quite unreal to have a strike before the next meeting. This did not go down well. Several around the table protested that preparations had gone too far. It was only then that Molyneaux realised that others had already been organising the day of action and he had been in blissful, if not deliberate, ignorance. Only then did he realise that there were those who were determined to hold such a protest "come hell or high water". This was a mistake on his part. He should have gauged the mood of the "senior" troops in both Unionist parties before then and have headed the "braves" off before they started on their war path.

He readily admits that both he and Paisley were mugged at this heated and angry three hour meeting. After it had ended he stood in another room and thought of resigning as party leader. He was hurt because he did not understand the reaction. It was still with him when he made the Assembly speech announcing the strike the following afternoon. He realised both of them had been humiliated and he stood questioning himself on what he should do. Both McCusker and Ross stood loyally by him, pointing out to others at the table that they had interpreted the talks incorrectly, but to no avail. He told Ross what he was thinking and was advised against any such move. He thinks now he was right to cling on. Possibly, by resigning, he would have been contributing to a greater state of chaos.

"At least if we stayed in the saddle we could keep control and avoid the wilder excesses which might otherwise have developed. Rightly or wrongly that was the decision." The *News Letter* the next morning described the turn around as a "Shock No to Maggie" and the newspaper said the statement issued after the Glengall Street meeting had emphasised that the two leaders would no longer talk to the Prime Minister which was in sharp contrast to the mood immediately after the Downing Street meeting. Even the statement was a bone of contention. Molyneaux wanted to delay it for 24 hours until everyone had calmed down. He was told in no uncertain terms that if he refused, others would ensure that the press heard what had happened at the meeting.

The terse statement was duly published. The two leaders said: "We will now proceed to discharge our election mandate and withdraw the consent of the people of Northern Ireland from this Government". Molyneaux went home mortified and depressed.

The next day began his attempts to curtail the "wilder excesses" with his Assembly speech as Downing Street said the Prime Minister had been astounded by the two Unionist leaders' statement and King noted "some very hot headed people may have been behind the leaders' change of heart".

After spelling out what had happened at Downing Street and pointing out that he had already briefed his party officers and Assembly members, Molyneaux said they all had a responsibility to ensure that there was some kind of discipline and co-ordination for the stoppage.

"The reason I have said that we have a responsibility is that there are various matters that have to be attended to. The first thing is that if it is going to be effective this must be a disciplined show of rejection and repudiation of the Agreement. It seems to me that with our network of control through the Province we are in a position to achieve that."

He went on: "We must make it quite clear that now that we are seeking to control and discipline this legitimate day of protest and of action, it is a democratic operation. There can be no place for any paramilitary or illegal form of action in the course of the operation and that is where we as elected representatives must shoulder our responsibility". He said there had to be four requirements – discipline, no hardship, no violence and no paramilitary or illegal activity. He warned that if responsibilities were not met then the Unionist cause would lose ground in the Western World.

His views were reiterated in the leaders' joint newspaper advertisement calling for support for the strike. In it Molyneaux said: "There must be no violence in the course of this operation on Monday. The protest must be rigidly controlled and any irresponsible people weeded out" while Paisley noted "This should be a passive and voluntary demonstration. Violence and intimidation can play no part in our plan. We do not want the support of those who do not accept this condition".

For the first time the co-ordinating body which had obviously been in operation before the Downing Street talks appeared in print. The 1986 Workers Committee called on their colleagues to support the strike. It was said to be chaired by Frank Leslie, an inarticulate DUP Belfast councillor. His party's deputy leader Peter Robinson described them as "responsible members of the community".

Molyneaux's curtailment exercise continued at a party executive committee meeting on February 28. The newspapers the following morning announced that the Ulster Unionist Party was attempting to open up a new front in dialogue on devolution. Millar, as general secretary, said the party was seeking an agenda for the aftermath of March 3's day of action. He said people wanted to know where they were going politically on the "morning after" the protest.

The executive had approved unanimously a package with two stages. The first would be between the Government and the constitutional parties in Northern Ireland to consider the Government proposals on devolution while the second would be dependent upon agreement between the governments in London and Dublin and a newly constituted government in Northern Ireland to confirm a new British/Irish framework.

The day of action or "loyalists letting off steam" to use a favourite phrase of Jim Prior's passed but it did untold damage to the anti-Agreement campaign. Molyneaux wrote to the Prime Minister on behalf of himself and Paisley on March 7. He pointed out that at each level of their parties the overwhelming view was that there had been no change in the situation since the signing of the Agreement the previous November.

However, he said, it remained their purpose to create the framework within which dialogue could take place. He enclosed the two resolutions and added that both leaders hoped the Prime Minister would look upon the proposals as a constructive development. It was exactly the same position as set out by the two leaders at the February 25 meeting but the opportunity had been lost. The two men had almost faced a vote of no confidence and Molyneaux had seriously considered resignation. The day of action, as the Ulster Unionist leader knew beforehand, achieved nothing. It was his own realisation that the "hot heads" as described by Tom King would find themselves in the same place after their strike that encouraged him to hold on and weather the storm. Most of those who vociferously advocated the stoppage such as Jim Allister and Frank Millar are no longer in politics. But they had lost any small initiative that they may have had thanks to those who had wanted to show "muscle".

A view which has become more prominent in Molyneaux's thinking has been that the Prime Minister was indeed bullied into and badly briefed on the actual details of the Agreement. At that February 25 meeting she was keen, he suggests, to find some means of seeking an alternative.

"I had said to her that I knew she recognised it as an international agreement between two sovereign governments and that she claimed they had a unique relationship. I told her that neither of us were suggesting that she talk directly to Dublin about the situation but there were channels through which she could sound out their attitude to the possible modification of the accord. We were not demanding the complete abolition of the agreement at that time. We wanted her to recognise that it had been a hideous blunder, that she should try to think it through with us and then try with her co-signatory to find a better way out."

Molyneaux was convinced at that time that the Irish Prime Minister Garret FitzGerald had been shocked at the strength of opposition to the accord and while he would not have relished it being dramatically altered, he felt the Dublin premier would have been willing to discuss alterations.

"I am not saying that it would have been entirely satisfactory. I am certainly not saying that it was going to be a cosmetic exercise which was going to buy us off. The situation was developing in such a horrific way for all of us – the two governments and ourselves – that it was worth exploring the possibility of making some change in the situation. If Dublin had been willing to co-operate with the Goverment then it is just possible that we might have achieved something."

But the day of action put paid to that and Molyneaux has his share of the blame for allowing it to go ahead.

9. The Long View

On June 29, 1988 the House of Commons held its fourteenth annual debate on the renewal of the Northern Ireland Act 1974. In it Jim Molyneaux described the ritual as a "phoney circus act" and noted with some saracasm: "We owe it to the honour of the House to consider whether we can, with any justification, continue to append the adjective 'temporary'. It is wearing a little thin after 14 years".

But he went on to welcome a speech made by the Labour Party's spokesman on Northern Ireland, Kevin McNamara, in which he repeated the Irish Taoiseach Charles Haughey's statement that the Anglo-Irish Agreement was not written in tablets of stone.

"That in itself is good news. However, the hon. Member for Kingston upon Hull, North (McNamara) went beyond that and, as I recollect, he said he was quite prepared to consider an alternative agreement, a wider and more workable agreement. The hon. Member for Antrim, North (Ian Paisley) will agree that he and I have been saying that privately and then publicly for ten months. We have said that our two parties are prepared to be positive. We are prepared to assist, to make our contribution to the design of a much wider, more workable and more practical agreement. We are genuine in saying that we regard such an agreement as a prerequisite. I hope that we can now persuade the Government to fall into line with the Opposition, with the three parties in the Dail and to say that they too, are prepared to be flexible and to consider a more workable agreement."

Over a year later at a Twelfth of July demonstration in Hillsborough, Molyneaux told Orangemen: "The waiting will soon be over. The voyage can soon begin". After almost four years he believed what he had described at the first massive Belfast City Hall rally as "staying power" was beginning to pay off: "Once freed from the burden of the dying diktat, we could and would co-operate with the Government to the betterment of the Ulster people". The forces which had supported the Union, he said, in contrast to the two governments, had remained rocklike in their determination to see "this thing through as a united people".

147

He again returned to use that work "rocklike" within a matter of weeks after he and Paisley had their first meeting with a new face at Stormont Castle, Peter Brooke, who had taken over as Secretary of State from Tom King. Molyneaux told waiting reporters after the private meeting that Unionists were on a solid rock and had no reason to move. It was up to the Government to get itself out of stormy waters.

The following day, on one of his first trips out in the new job, Mr Brooke informed journalists, in County Tyrone, that both governments were prepared to consider an alternative to the accord. This comment immediately received denials, from the SDLP in the North and Southern politicians, including the former Foreign Affairs Minister Peter Barry. However, in spite of the ensuing exchange of words one person remained silent, the Irish Prime Minister Charles Haughey. It was the Taoiseach who insisted that paragraph twenty nine of the review of the accord, published in late May, be included. Instructions were issued to the Dublin negotiating team that they were to be emphatic about its insertion. There had been a change in attitude by the Irish Government. In early 1988 there were expressions of surprise when Haughey began to express the view that he wanted to build a relationship with Unionists. Molyneaux replied, amid some calls that he was becoming a traitor, by suggesting that policy papers could be exchanged. The door for quiet diplomacy was opened.

The review which Unionists had made clear they would not become involved in, had got underway after the third anniversary of the Agreement. The thirty paragraph document which looked at the workings of the Anglo-Irish conference, then took six months to complete.

But to Molyneaux the important paragraph was that No. 29. It read: "If, in future, it were to appear that the objectives of the Agreement could be more effectively served by changes in the scope and nature of the working of the conference, consistent with the basic provisions and spirit of the Agreement, the two governments would be ready in principle to consider such changes".

To him, the fact that the two governments had agreed on the wording of this paragraph which indicated that they would consider variations, then it would be a logical, small step to announce publicly that they were prepared to consider an alternative. He returned to this hope in a speech as Sovereign Grand Master of the Royal Black Institution at the end of August. He suggested that a "deliverance" could come within a matter of months once the British and Irish governments matched what he described as the flexibility and statesmanship of Russian leader Mikhail Gorbachev.

He had witnessed a subtle change in attitudes towards the Agreement over the previous weeks. The London Independent, in an editorial, noted: "The best strategy for the Government is to consolidate its gains, especially ensuring a maximum of justice for the Roman Catholic population and to refrain from further dramatic initiatives such as the Anglo-Irish Agreement of 1985. That enraged the Protestant majority by enshrining in principle that the Republic had a legitimate interest in the affairs of Northern Ireland, and it may have given the IRA the false impression that withdrawal was at hand. Northern Ireland is destined to remain part of the United Kingdom for the foreseeable future, and should be administered with the same standards of justice as the mainland".

SDLP leader John Hume also advocated a small shift in the nationalist psychological make-up. In a speech to the Merriman Summer School in County Clare he called on nationalists to play a constructive role in Northern Ireland society. It was no longer enough, he said, to nurse one's alienation or sense of grievance and continued: "I make this point not to downplay the reality of injustice or discrimination but it strikes me that one of the challenges facing nationalists in the north today is how to play a constructive, rather than a hostile or passive role in society".

While he hit out at the Unionist leadership for its attitudes to the Agreement, he went on: "It is crucial to recognise that in spite of the legitimacy of our past grievances the world does not forever owe us a living and that, given equality of treatment, we should not only be quite capable, but anxious to stand on our own feet and use our talents in playing a positive and constructive role in society than indulging in the negative comfort of the grievance mentality".

To Molyneaux the building of trust between the two communities, added to the attitude as outlined by Hume, would create proper progress in Northern Ireland. The relationship built up by Hume, Molyneaux and Paisley over the fight to save Harland and Wolff shipyard in Belfast and its transfer to the private sector, reflected their own growing trust. However the ever cautious Molyneaux highlighted how some people then take such a step out of context: "People have pointed out, from both sides of the Irish Sea, that they were very impressed that the three main party leaders could come together and present the case for the shipyard's survival to the Prime Minister. But they then go on to say 'well, if you can work at that level, why can't you get into a higher initiative'. What they should be saying is 'Right, you were able to do that and it came off, why can't you keep on doing that'.

It would be much more constructive than trying to reach for the unattainable.

"I do not think you can wave a wand at the end of twenty years and obliterate all the bitterness, the tension and the antagonism and make something work overnight. You cannot do it by saying that as from next Monday morning we are going to have some new super structure set up because unless the support is there below the participants, then they are going to be left with no visible means of such support and the whole thing will simply collapse."

In that same speech to Blackmen in Killylea, County Armagh, he made a comparison between Northern Ireland and the changing attitudes in Poland and the Baltic states: "Fifty years ago the signing of the Stalin/Hitler pact decided the fate of Poland, Estonia, Latvia and Lithuania without consultation with those who had to live with the consequences. Their plea for their right to decide how they would be governed fell upon deaf ears and the diktat was imposed without regard to the democratic wishes of those unfortunate people. At long last those victims are able to assert their rights because the world is a changed place".

He claimed the British Isles was paying lip service to democracy as the two sovereign powers had sought to impose their joint diktat without consultation and without the consent of those who had to live with the consequences.

He continues with the comparison in conversations: "In those four countries people have kept their heads and said that they better not aim too high to begin with as the whole movement could be brought down around their heads. A further aspect is that there are people outside, those in high places, who are urging caution, emphasising that it will work out in the end and advising that these people should be modest in their demands.

"But these are the very same people who are saying to us in Northern Ireland, 'We are not satisfied with what you are doing at local level, please sit down around the table at Stormont and we will even fly you in and out by helicopter to add to the drama. We will get everyone stating all their demands and hey presto we will get it to work'. They are giving the advice to the Poles which they ought to be giving to us. We ought to be, at least, allowed the same privilege as the Poles to judge the pace at which we can bring about political change in Northern Ireland."

His "long road" advice to see the Anglo-Irish Agreement placed on a shelf has been dominated by many antics, including MPs going to jail. He readily admits that there were mistakes – the violence, the intimidation of police families and the way in which some councils, primarily Belfast, found themselves embroiled in a legal battle over their protests.

However he believes the vocal and vivid opposition was a necessary element in the Unionist campaign against the accord. He realised that no single protest was going to change the two governments' minds. By maintaining this view he had to prove, on many occasions immediately after the signing, to party members that this was the right one to hold. On many occasions it took a lot of convincing.

"I knew no single activity or demonstration would bring down the Agreement. Even all of them put together would not end the Agreement in the sense that it would secure its ceremonial burning. I felt and am now convinced looking back on it, that we were right to demonstrate, not only the lack of consent, but the vehement opposition to it. I believe that prevented the implementation and the extension of the original plans which were in the minds of the draftsmen in Whitehall and Dublin.

The protest was justified and it has been as effective as it could have been given that no government, still less two, will ever admit publicly that they have made a mistake. The whole range of protests, the fact that the pro-Union majority remains as opposed to the Agreement as they ever were, although they do not go around every day saying so, has achieved a definite slowing up of the implementation of the Agreement." He does not see this as propaganda but fact and believes through his conversations with people across Northern Ireland that while the resentment is silent it is still sullen.

There was an even deeper sense of indignation and protests were still prominent in the wake of the March 3 day of action in 1986. Molyneaux and Paisley did their best to mop up the damage done to their campaign by the ensuing violence.

In his annual report for that year the RUC Chief Constable Sir John Hermon pointed out that there were 500 attacks on homes and 120 families had been forced to flee. He described 1986 as a "most extraordinarily difficult time". He recognised that there had been a "deep seated opposition" to the accord which added to the political impasse and that his force had faced massive public order problems.

The Ulster Unionist leader recognised that a slide to widespread disturbances would do nothing to help the pro-Union cause and bitterly condemned the attacks on RUC and Catholic homes when he spoke in the Assembly on April 23, 1986.

"I want to put on record the plea that anyone who may be tempted to plan or lend assistance to those engaged in, acts of violence should stay his hand. The democratic processes have not yet been exhausted. We, and the people who are so tempted, owe it to the province of Ulster and its people to take all constructive steps possible and to refrain from any action that would cause further loss of life or damage or would harm or destroy the destiny of Northern Ireland."

It was almost six months after the signing of the accord and the two Unionist leaders, with the joint working party, were attempting to put the anti-Agreement campaign back on the rails before it did degenerate further into nothing more than nightly sectarian attacks. Just 24 hours previously, after a protest march in the massive housing estate of Rathcoole in Newtownabbey, police vehicles were petrol bombed and Catholic homes attacked.

The two leaders announced a twelve point package which they described as the "rationalisation, updating and consolidation" of the protest. It included a rates strike were they advised the community to "withhold and delay" the payment; education and health board members were asked to adjourn meetings as were district councillors and the boycotting of Parliament by Unionist MPs would continue. The announcement received an appeal from Law and Order Minister Nicholas Scott who called on opponents of the Agreement not to be drawn into illegal activity. But Molyneaux maintains the rates strike was a "valuable" aspect of the Unionist campaign.

"I backed it because people were not being asked not to pay, they were simply being told to withhold their payments. It did have an impact, particularly during the first year, because the Government was deprived of that steady income. It also caused Ministers some irritation because it was another manifestation of the fact that the rank and file people were prepared to take that action. I remember when I appeared at court in Antrim, I asked permission to speak and the magistrate said of course I could as I was not there on a criminal charge. I did not accept that part of the protest reluctantly as I felt it was a legitimate way for people to protest, not to let off steam, but to demonstrate to the Government that they opposed the Agreement."

Early in the opposition campaign the Assembly decided with its Unionist majority that it would not continue with its scrutinising role over proposed Government legislation. The ten man Alliance team left and the Stormont chamber became a Unionist talking shop. By May it was clear the Government was going to pull down the shutters on the body which had become nothing more than a platform for anti-Agreement outpourings. The day before Secretary of State Tom King announced in the House of Commons that it would be dissolved, Ian

Paisley ironically told the remaining Assembly members: "I sat in this place when it was a Parliament, and it was closed down. I sat in the previous Assembly and it was closed down. I sat in the Northern Ireland Convention which, after submitting its report, was terminated. They may close this House down, but they cannot close down the indomitable spirit of loyal Ulster".

Molyneaux, as usual, was less impassioned in his speech which was his last major contribution to the doomed Assembly. He pointed out that there were those in Government who were looking around for reasons to close the body down and had fallen across one which said that the Assembly had failed in its primary role.

"Contrary to what the Northern Ireland Office is saying, its primary role was to achieve a stable form of devolved government. That was the main objective of our being elected to the Northern Ireland Assembly. But you may remember Mr Speaker, that we put forward the view in the House of Commons that the 1982 Act made that impossible. It is no use blaming the members of the Northern Ireland Assembly for that. In the Act Mr Prior raised the hurdles so high that progress of any kind was impossible. Members will recall the three main hurdles: firstly, the seventy per cent figure (this had to be gained amongst members if any powers were to be devolved to the body); secondly widespread support in the Assembly; and, thirdly – and this was a very neat one – widespread support in the community. That third hurdle took out of the hands of the Northern Ireland Assembly the power to come to any conclusion on any form of devolved government, as it remained open to an unnamed group of individuals to say 'Never mind what the elected representatives have said. We do not agree with this proposed form of devolved government'. The Secretary of State was bound, not just on a whim, as to whether he liked it or not but by the Act, to take account of such an objection when deciding whether the Northern Ireland Assembly had made a prudent decision."

He reiterated that because there was to be no suspension of the accord to allow dialogue to take place that neither he nor Paisley could enter into "any negotiations whatsoever". He rejected the mounting calls for the two leaders to begin talks, claiming the "great and the good" who were urging such movement were mistaken.

"With respect, I say that they are mistaken. As far as I am concerned – and that goes for the hon. Member for North Antrim as well – that day will not be reached until the Anglo-Irish Agreement is done away with for good. We do not have to talk. It is the responsibility of the Government – as it is of any government – to govern. They must govern by the authority of their countrymen who elected them and not by the authority of any foreign government."

Within a month the Stormont talking shop was closed – in spite of an address to the Queen from its members and a motion to the clerk of the Privy Council. On June 23 the Speaker, North Down MP Jim Kilfedder announced he had received a letter from Mr King's private secretary and read it to the members. It informed them that the Queen, that afternoon, had made the Northern Ireland Assembly (Dissolution) Order 1986 which came into operation forthwith. Mr Kilfedder left the chair at 3.54 pm, DUP members and two Ulster Unionists Fraser Agnew and Jeffrey Donaldson were removed in the early hours of the following morning by RUC officers who had to carry each one from the chamber.

After a summer which was again peppered with violence, particularly in Portadown, by September the two leaders felt the opposition – especially in council chambers – was beginning to drift again. They had separate meetings with councillor representatives with each urging a toughening up of tactics. In reply the members agreed to continue with their adjournment policies but refused to back a total boycott or a mass resignation.

Molyneaux returned to this theme at a second Belfast City Hall rally to mark the first anniversary of the accord. Again organisers worried about the numbers game but it was estimated that even more people appeared. However this time the event was marred by masked youths who went on the rampage as soon as Ian Paisley went forward to speak. Unknown to the majority of the crowd who could not see them, they broke shop windows and looted stores before being charged by police.

The Ulster Unionist leader, before the violence broke out, informed his audience that the greatest achievement in their campaign so far had been the demonstration that there was no consent for the Anglo-Irish Agreement in Northern Ireland and went on to outline how the protest was to expand. He admitted that the adjournment policy in councils had reached the end of the road and certain alternatives would be put to councillors. A petition would be sent to the Queen; all Unionists would be told to resign from statutory boards and Government agencies; Parliamentary activity would not be resumed and more revenues would be withheld.

There was little reaction within both Unionist parties' ranks to the proposals. While some DUP members maintained the measures were not strong enough, a growing number in the Ulster Unionist ranks were wary of resigning from any body. Molyneaux's own authority was questioned when, on November 26, his councillors voted not to resign from councils – in spite of his support for such action.

"I was conscious of the fact members of councils and membership of boards did mean a great deal to people, not for the honour and glory, but that they did feel they were contributing to the community. I knew they were being expected to be put to the torch and I realised there was the possibility that they might not do it. But then I had to put myself in the position. I had to say to myself, 'look if we allow the Agreement to take root and flourish then some day these people will see that membership of boards is quite irrelevant as the person sitting next to them is an appointee suggested first of all by Dublin'.

I felt that if I did not give the leadership and recommend resignation then that situation could well have developed. It was not a command telling people that they had to follow hardliners and the working party for them to keep their places. It was a genuine view that we had to demonstrate that if protests were not made then the Northern Ireland Office would have gone further down the road and rather than appoint councillors, they would have given places to Dublin nominees which they could do under the terms of the Agreement." Few paid any attention to his call and only a trickle of members actually resigned from boards.

He recognised the risk involved and was again accused of being ineffectual: "But if I had gone along with them and taken the soft option then would they have had any more respect for me? I think not. I was in the position of saying 'Look, this is how seriously I view the situation and this is what I think you should do.' It put them on the spot and made it crystal clear where I stood. I was well aware that I would receive flak for it, particularly when they rejected the advice".

Over the next few months councillors continued with their adjournment policy applied in different ways across Northern Ireland until Unionist councillors in Belfast were faced with court action and fined £25,000 for failing to resume normal business. Castlereagh Borough Council soon faced similar action as the Department of the Environment appointed a Commissioner to strike a rate in loyalist controlled councils. It took until October 1987 before the Belfast members agreed to pay their fine and a further £11,000 in costs over their mishandled protest before they faced surcharges and disqualification.

"I told the councillors who attended that meeting which rejected the resignation proposal that they had to work out an alternative. I warned them that as a consequence of their decision they could be putting themselves in danger of facing a surcharge and an eventual ban on holding public office. It did not seem to dawn on them at the time that that was the risk they were running."

The new year of 1987 heralded the loyal petition to the Queen for a referendum on the Agreement but it had little impact, in spite of the organisers claiming they had gathered 400,000 signatures within a month. Ideas of how to graphically show that the Unionist opposition had not dwindled were beginning to appear thin on the ground.

The next was to latch onto new Public Order legislation which had already gone through in England and Wales. However there were differences with the Northern Ireland Order and Unionist politicians found it easy to blame the Agreement and the Irish Government's alleged input into the legislation for bringing about such changes. They were relatively minor and in some cases the English legislation was stricter, but what the Northern Ireland Order did do was to give the Chief Constable more scope as to how he was going to apply the letter of the law.

The two Unionist leaders called for peaceful demonstrations on April 11 but 24 hours earlier they, with nine colleagues, took to the streets of Belfast in their own illegal parade. Molyneaux, with his brown envelope briefcase under one arm and a poster declaring Free Speech in the other, walked from the City Hall to a central police station to hand in a letter of protest against the legislation. Paisley had already exchanged bitter words with the UDA who had made it clear that it would not be involved in any of the demonstrations and advised other loyalists to do the same.

He noted: "If people are afraid to take the penalty for defying this dictatorial law, that is just too bad, I'm not afraid. I have never asked anyone to do anything I would not do myself". The paramilitary organisation replied by pointing out that the DUP leader had always managed to be abroad during critical periods in Northern Ireland's history. But he was there for the MPs protest, those missing were the Strangford MP John Taylor, the North Down member Jim Kilfedder and the South Down representative Enoch Powell. During the short march they were warned by the police that they were breaking the law and could be summoned. Molyneaux handed in the protest letter and wryly told waiting reporters that even their own union, the National Union of Journalists, had been opposed to the English legislation. The next day's demonstrations were a flop with small turnouts across the country. It was the last significant call made by the two Unionist leaders for major demonstrations against the accord.

The illegal marchers were duly summoned, made a court appearance in December 1987 and refused to pay their £50 fines. Each then faced a few days imprisonment – apart from Jim Molyneaux who had a mysterious benefactor.

In spite of mutterings of disapproval from Parliamentary friends about Unionist MPs who had already been behind bars for not paying taxes, Molyneaux had approved of the course of action. He felt cheated when he learnt a few days before his planned arrest that a solicitor's firm in Craigavon had paid his fine. He still does not know at whose instigation and believes it was done deliberately to embarrass him. The Unionist leader felt the protest was right as his members, because of Northern Ireland's legislation being passed by Order in Council, had been denied the privilege afforded to other MPs to amend the English law as it went through its Parliamentary stages: "Our Members of Parliament having failed to get the law amended and knowing what was at stake, had a duty to put their money where their mouths were and face the consequences".

His own personal protest, much to the annoyance of the Lord Chancellor Lord Hailsham, was to resign the Justice of the Peace position he had held for some 20 years. He had found the work interesting and of particular help as he was also vice-chairman of the Muckamore Abbey eastern special care management committee where he had to chair disciplinary hearings. It also taught him to be cautious in all that he said.

He derived great satisfaction out of being "open house" to the wider community when individuals asked for references or they needed him to witness a private document. As is in human nature, most people tended to want to tell him what was in their confidential papers but he always tried to persuade them not to and had a habit of placing a blotter over the document, only leaving room for his signature. "I enjoyed it as you were able to do a variety of things for people, it certainly wasn't because you had letters after your name."

His entry into Parliament meant he was less and less available for court work which eventually stopped, but he was able to carry on the "open house" aspect of the voluntary job. He decided to resign the position on what he felt were perfectly legitimate grounds: "In my letter to the Lord Chancellor I informed him that I had taken the oath as a Justice of the Peace to enforce the law of the Crown and Parliament within the Queen's realm. It had never been my intention to enforce a law made with the assistance of a foreign government".

He received a blistering letter in return from the Lord Chancellor who informed him that it was disgraceful that he had seen fit to use an office bestowed by the Queen for his own political ends. Lord Hailsham emphatically told him that under no circumstances was he going to submit his name for resignation to the Queen. Molyneaux persisted and further letters were exchanged with those from the Unionist leader pointing out certain oversights on the part of the Lord Chancellor's office. Eventually, after several months, he received a cordial letter from London, informing him that his resignation would indeed be put forward.

During the early months of 1987, the clamour for some initiative grew. As obvious opposition of the Agreement waned, more and more people from church leaders to industrialists urged the Unionist politicians to do something rather than "say no". They were spurred on in their task when the UDA, under the guidance of John McMichael, published its document "Common Sense" which called for a constitutional conference to be set up. This it hoped would lead to a devolved assembly and a coalition government based on party strengths. It received a warm welcome from a diverse selection of community leaders, including the Catholic hierarchy.

In the face of such calls the two Unionist leaders appointed, in late February, a Unionist Task Force. It had two main objectives: to secure support for the continuing campaign against the Anglo-Irish Agreement and to ascertain what consensus, if any, existed about alternatives to the Agreement. The three man team – Harold McCusker, Peter Robinson and Frank Millar – were to report back to the two leaders after consultations had been completed.

Their discussions included talks with church leaders, the loyal institutions, the Ulster Clubs and the Confederation of British Industry. A draft document was drawn up and discussed by the team and the two leaders during a lengthy, confidential meeting at Westminster. The team went back to the drawing board and what they described as an "abridged" version "An End to Drift" was put on display to the public in June. It proposed the creation of a Unionist Convention to construct and lead a renewed campaign of protest. This body would also be invited to endorse the demand for an alternative to and replacement of the accord.

It appealed to the two leaders to draw public notice to plans and proposals they had offered in the past as a basis for negotiation. The team suggested that these should include the Catherwood plan in which both Unionist parties had abandoned pure majority rule as the price for devolution and the leaders' correspondence with the Prime Minister in the autumn of 1985 in which they had pledged their willingness to negotiate a British/Irish framework for the promotion of better relationships within Ireland. The report warned that in advance of any negotiations failure to arrive at the consensus would leave the Unionist leadership no alternative but to seek an entirely new base for Northern Ireland outside the present constitutional context. The three man team, however, offered no precise or definite suggestion as to what the alternative might be although they said that while devolved government within the context of the UK was their objective, it would be "wise and prudent" for Unionists to anticipate that it might not be.

There was a warm reception for the report from the wider community. But it then appeared to them that the two leaders were "hedging their bets" and were avoiding straight answers on the contents of the document. Both would only say that they would study it carefully before making any comments. To many it seemed the report had already been shelved.

Molyneaux had one major problem with the report. The Unionist Convention was to include all shades of opinion and that included the UDA. This he could not tolerate.

In a speech, on return to the House of Commons after the June 1987 General Election in which his party lost the South Down seat to the SDLP, he referred to the report and the criticism which he and Paisley were facing over their apparent stalling on a reply.

"If there is to be any prospect of success in our endeavours, by which I mean feeling our way forward, this time cautiously; not engaging in any high wire acts, but building solidly on constructive approaches and workable and realistic suggestions, there must be a degree of confidentiality. When public representatives are placed in positions of responsibility – and many of us are bearing a burden we never sought – they must be guided by a degree of consideration and caution. They must also be granted a degree of authority to act on their own judgement, because presumably that is why we are all elected in the first place. We must always remember that if we are to carry with us our electorate and those to whom we are responsible, we must retain our integrity and never knowingly betray the trust reposed in us."

He had been pressed by the Newry/Armagh MP Seamus Mallon to give his reaction to the report and he replied: "What I have just said relates to the judgement that the hon. Member for Antrim North

(Paisley) and I must exercise as we sympathetically evaluate the suggestions in the report 'An End to Drift'. We must then judge the timing, order and priority that we attach to the various suggestions contained in the report of our three colleagues to whom I have publicly paid tribute and I repeat that tribute now". The following day, July 8, the two men announced they would use the report in low level introductory talks with civil servants.

During this period Molyneaux not only had to face the accusation that two old, bitter men were leading the Unionist parties nowhere and there had to be a change in leadership but also that he was Paisley's puppet. His single mindedness is shown in that he took pleasure out of the taunt. To him it meant the campaign was working and that this accusation was a deliberate attempt to split the Unionist pact.

"It amused me. In fact it encouraged me because it meant that our opponents were exasperated because of the unity between the two parties and were doing their damnest to break it up. They thought one of the effective ways was to say to my people 'this man of yours is a stooge, why don't you elect a man of iron who will stand up to Paisley'. It caused me a great deal of amusement because I knew what they were up to and anyway, whatever people think of me, in a curious way I seem to be less hurt by such criticism than others. Politicians seem to confess in their memoirs or in private conversations that they were upset by an attack made on them by someone in the House of Commons. It does not ever hurt me. I just shrug it off and simply say I have a job to do, I have decided that this is the right thing to do and I'm damned if they are going to turn me from the course I have embarked on.

If you are going to be as thin skinned as that then you should not be a politician. I am not saying it is a virtue, maybe it is a degree of insensitivity but I used to chuckle at all the cartoons of Big Ian and Wee Jim. Even if there were other accusations, the first thing I asked myself was 'well, why are they doing that' and when I realised why then I'd say to myself 'right, the more the merrier'. Then you go on doing what they are trying to criticise you for as you then know it has hit home. But this sense of hurt is something I am oddly conscious of in others. It is not that I am any better than them, but I would never unnecessarily insult a Government Minister or any other politician. It is pointless for one thing and secondly you always have at the back of your mind that they are human beings, that they are going to be hurt and that things between you will never be the same again."

This immunity has always been in his character. He can never remember being particularly sensitive about what people said about

him or what they thought of him. However there is one Achilles heel:
"If it was something where you made a proper mess of a situation and
you were already feeling down and someone comes along and points it
out to you. Well, then that does hit home because you know they are
right and it does hurt".

The Unionist MPs had returned to Westminster following the
election to greetings from all sides of the House. However they had lost
Enoch Powell in South Down and the overall figures showed a drop in
the total Unionist poll. This was in spite of them having a joint
manifesto. Their shares went down by 2.3 per cent to 54.8 per cent.
Critics claimed the wider community was fed up with antics and wanted
some kind of political movement.

Molyneaux referred to this when he spoke in the House on July 7 in
the debate on the renewal of the Northern Ireland Act 1974. It was in
this speech too that he spoke of the Task Force report. He took on
board points made by the Foyle MP John Hume and continued: "If he
is referring to working together in Northern Ireland at an initially
modest administrative level without the involvement of any foreign
government, I do not think that there would be any great difficulty. The
hon. Gentleman and members of his party sit on the Bench before me,
the SDLP playing their part and performing a full role as an Opposition
Party in this sovereign Parliament of the UK. I agree with the hon.
Member for Foyle that there should not be any difficulty in starting to
think and talk about the possibility of a modest start in what the hon.
Gentleman termed 'administration at some level', not in the oversight
of the Anglo-Irish diktat".

During that same debate the Secretary of State emphasised that the
Government was ready to listen to constructive ideas from any quarter
and without preconditions: "It is in the interests of all the people in the
Province for the talking to start soon".

It did, soon afterwards on July 14, with senior civil servants,
including the head of the service in Northern Ireland Sir Kenneth
Bloomfield. By September enough of the ground rules had been
established to allow Tom King to join the discussions. The Stormont
statement afterwards read: "The purpose of these meetings has been to
clarify the circumstances in which talks about talks may develop into
wider ranging political negotiations. Officials reporting on these
exchanges to the Secretary of State, recommended that he should meet
the leaders personally to hear their views directly. The Secretary of
State accordingly joined today's meeting for that purpose. Another
meeting is expected in October".

The *News Letter* leader the following morning, September 15, noted: "As Mr Molyneaux said after the session it was inevitable that the two civil servants would eventually feel that they had to have advice from the head of the department. The overwhelming majority of people in Northern Ireland have absolute confidence that Mr Molyneaux and Mr Paisley will do what is right by them and by the province. The most important weapon in their armour – in fact many would say the only viable one – is the trust and confidence of the Unionist people".

The slow process continued until a round of talks at the Northern Ireland Office in London pre-Christmas 1987. At it the Secretary of State agreed that he would consider a paper to be drawn up by the two Unionist leaders over the holiday period which would outline what had taken place. But it was more than that. It was presented to him on January 26 as the Unionist alternative to the Anglo-Irish Agreement and included a devolved administration with a committee system and with their chairmen being elected on a proportional basis. To Molyneaux and Paisley it meant that the Government could no longer say that Unionists had not been constructive. But the document was never released for public consumption and the Government has never felt it necessary to make a formal reply to it. The two Unionist leaders held two further meetings with the NIO team but by May 1988 there seemed little purpose in their continuing and they ended.

Molyneaux's stance on the talks about talks has not changed. His views on that alternative and the way internal progress could be made in Northern Ireland have not altered. It is similar to the position he took up over the Atkins round table conference. Party colleagues expressed amazement after he returned from his meeting with the Prime Minister in November 1979 that in spite of literally being surrounded by senior civil servants, Mrs Thatcher, her Parliamentary Private Secretary Ian Gow and Humphrey Atkins, he refused to budge. To him the Conservative party was divorcing itself from its election manifesto pledge on Northern Ireland and he would have nothing to do with it. He had rationally come to that decision and he felt confident his party would eventually understand why.

In characteristic fashion he did not thump the table but subtly asked the Prime Minister as to when she was going to consult the Leader of the Opposition over the new trade union laws. When she replied, that the reforms had been set out in the manifesto and she had no need to consult the Labour Party, he quietly replied it was for the same reason that he would not go to the round table talks. The Conservatives' proposals on Northern Ireland had been set out in the manifesto and the Government should not need to consult anyone as to how they were to be implemented.

"As Humphrey read out his statement in the House of Commons on the creation of the talks, I was sitting there thinking the opposite. They have now turned their backs on the Neave/Thatcher policy. Why are they doing this? They are doing it because there can be no place for Washington or Dublin in the Neave plan for an administration council so they want something now to allow their participation. That is betrayal of Neave and Thatcher herself therefore I decided I was not going.

It is resolve I suppose, but it is resolve based on calculation. It is not based on some impulse. In the aftermath of refusing to go, all hell broke loose and pressures were applied from all quarters. You simply had to stick it out. You had to keep saying to yourself 'I know what they are up to and it is not right and therefore I am having nothing to do with it'."

He sees a parallel between that and the Unionist opposition to the Anglo-Irish Agreement: "If we had weakened at any stage as far as the accord is concerned and had been seen to consent, we would have thrown away our position. The situation is changing in Poland and the Baltic States and it appears the process is continuing. But you cannot go on having people preach about free elections and heeding the message of the ballot box and then find Her Majesty's Government is governing the kindgom which prides itself on democracy, defying the ballot box as far as Northern Ireland is concerned. On principle you have to be absolutely rigid and ensure that you do not touch the pitch because if you do then you are finished".

The establishment of the Agreement, in a perverse way he believes, has helped Unionists recognise and begin to understand what he terms as their enemy. In his view, most Unionists misunderstood the reason why parliaments were established in Belfast and Dublin in 1920.

"Whitehall which at that time was heavily influenced by Lloyd George, meant there to be home rule institutions which would drift out of the orbit of the UK and maybe, some day, drift into one unit. But what they were really aiming for was that they would get away completely from Great Britain. Carson knew what they were up to and resisted it fiercely. In several speeches in the House of Commons, he pleaded with them not to do it but he lost the battle. He then had to accept Stormont as the price for staying out of a united Ireland.

"Craig, with Carson's support, fashioned Stormont into an instrument which, at most, could not be used against Unionists. He was well aware that Westminster was still the sovereign Parliament and what it did it could undo. Craig never made the mistake of our latter day Prime Ministers in imagining that they were involved in a fellow sovereign government. He was aware that the rug could be pulled from under him at any given time. Stormont did not strengthen the Union, in the sense that it was something which could be removed at any time, but he made certain it was not going to become a Home Rule Parliament and used against that very Union.

When Whitehall and Dublin realised that Stormont would not serve their end they could not do very much at the start until the Troubles began in 1969. That gave them the opportunity they had been waiting to undo the mistake they had made with the 1920 Act. They cold bloodedly decided as far back as then that Stormont would have to go. It was not just a snap decision by Ted Heath but plans were laid, I am convinced, as early as the 1930s, because Craig was making sure that Stormont was subservient to Westminster and not an independent institution on its own.

That is why he is convinced Unionists were wrong to continually look at Stormont and believe that it strengthened the Union. To him it did the reverse, particularly as successive Unionist Governments began to create what they regarded as an equal Parliament. He believes, by doing so, they played into Whitehall's hands. The real power lay at Westminster and that is why he, throughout his political life, has attempted to use that system within its rules. This is why he has been labelled on integrationist within his own community. The quiet man working at Westminster, within the sovereign parliament's etiquette, has not suited the Unionist community who believed that by having a building on a hill on the outskirts of Belfast somehow secured their heritage.

Whitehall has been determined ever since that it was not going to make the same mistake again and that is why they have spent the past 20 years trying to create what they regard, and people ought to open their eyes and regard, as a puppet Parliament, rather than regarding it as a sovereign means of governing themselves."

To him another attempt was the 1985 Agreement: "The difference about the Agreement was that it was so blatant. Its weakness was that it was so obvious that even the most moderate pro-Union person was incensed. What was worse for Whitehall was that it exposed, for the very first time, what they had been up to for such a long period. The scales dropped from everybody's eyes. At the first rally at the City Hall, the crowd did not have to be told what it all meant, they did not have to be told this is the working out of all the conspiracy theories that they had heard about. They could see it in plain black and white. In that sense the Anglo-Irish Agreement educated the rank and file in a way in which some of us had failed to do over ten years. It was positive help for us".

Because of this "re-education" he is convinced Northern Ireland will remain part of the UK – the only way it will not is if Unionists push themselves out of it.

"I have said at meetings where there has been a wide range of age that even the youngest in the hall would never live to see the day when Northern Ireland would be thrust out of the United Kingdom. The only way the end will come is if the Unionist people jump off the cliff themselves. I am now more convinced of that than I was even two years ago because everyone now sees what is involved and will think with greater clarity in the future."

9.4.